WORDS THAT CHANGED THE WORLD

UNDERSTANDING
THE DECLARATION
OF INDEPENDENCE

STEPHANIE SCHWARTZ DRIVER

ROSEN
PUBLISHING®

New York

This edition published in 2011 by:

The Rosen Publishing Group, Inc.
29 East 21st Street
New York, NY 10010

Library of Congress Cataloging-in-Publication Data

Driver, Stephanie Schwartz.
  Understanding the Declaration of Independence / Stephanie Schwartz Driver.
      p. cm.—(Words that changed the world)
  Includes bibliographical references and index.
  ISBN 978-1-4488-1669-9 (library binding)
  1. United States. Declaration of Independence. 2. United States—Politics and government—1775–1783. 3. United States—Politics and government—Philosophy. I. Title.
  E221.D76 2010
  973.3'13—dc22

                                                                                      2010010371

Manufactured in the United States of America

CPSIA Compliance Information: Batch #S10YA: For further information, contact Rosen Publishing, New York, New York, at 1-800-237-9932.

Text and design copyright © 2004 by The Ivy Press. This edition of *Manifesto: The Declaration of Independence* originally published in 2004 is published by arrangement with The Ivy Press Limited.

Picture credits
The author and publisher are grateful to the following for permission to reproduce illustrations:

Bridgeman Art Library, London: pp. 39T Birmingham Museum and Art Gallery, 39R Townley Hall Art Gallery and Museum, Burnley, 55 Roger-
      Viollet, 83 Visual Arts Library, London.
Cameron Collection: pp. 15, 18T, 68, 69.
Corbis: pp. 6 Ted Spiegel, 16 Dave G. Houser, 18L Freelance Photographers' Guild, 24, 28 Scott T. Smith, 30 Marc Muench, 52 Dave Bartruff, 54
      Kevin Fleming, 65 Minnesota Historical Society, 81 Burstein Collection, 82 Archivo Iconografico, 85 Asian Art and Architecture, 91T Craig
      Lovell, 100 Corcoran Gallery, 104, 107 Richard Cummins, 108 Flip Schulke, 111 David H. Wells.
Corbis/Bettmann Archive: pp. 7, 23, 41, 62, 64, 66, 86, 91R, 92.
Library of Congress Prints and Photographs Division: pp. 10, 11, 14, 17, 18L, 20, 21, 25, 27, 40, 43, 44, 45, 51, 53, 56, 76L, 76T, 80, 84, 88,
      94, 97, 98, 99, 101, 102L, 102T, 105, 112.

CONTENTS

UNDERSTANDING THE DECLARATION OF INDEPENDENCE
INTRODUCTION

The first official action of this nation declared the foundation of government in these words: "We hold these truths to be self-evident, that all men are created equal, that they are endowed by their Creator with certain unalienable rights, that among these are life, liberty and the pursuit of happiness." While such declaration of principles may not have the force of organic law, or be made the basis of judicial decision as to the limits of right and duty . . . it is always safe to read the letter of the Constitution in the spirit of the Declaration of Independence. No duty rests more imperatively upon the courts than the enforcement of those constitutional provisions intended to secure that equality of rights which is the foundation of free government.

U.S. Supreme Court, in Cotting v. Godard, 183 U.S. 79 (1901)

The Declaration of Independence, and Independence Hall, where it was signed, are emblems of the tumultuous creation of the United States as an independent nation.

The Declaration of Independence is the spiritual cornerstone of the United States. In its first few sentences it established the goals of a modern, democratic society—goals to which America, like many other countries, still aspires. Although it has no legal weight, the ethos of the Declaration of Independence underlies even constitutional law. The Justices of the Supreme Court, both liberal and conservative, avowedly keep the ideas of the Declaration in mind when making judgments—as they have done for two centuries.

Today the Declaration is considered one of America's three Charters of Freedom, proudly displayed with the Constitution and the Bill of Rights in the National Archives.

Ironically, at the time of its composition the Declaration had no such ambitions. Rather, it was essentially a press release, composed to spread the word both at home and abroad that the Continental Congress had voted for independence and to win support for the American cause.

This illustration, depicting the signing of the Declaration of Independence and celebrating the nation's founding fathers, was produced around 1856, at a time when Abraham Lincoln was evoking the Declaration in his campaigning speeches.

At its first readings in towns and villages throughout the newly independent colonies, the Declaration was celebrated, and then virtually forgotten for the next 50 years. Our exalted view of the text of the Declaration—or at least of its first few paragraphs—is due to Thomas Jefferson's stylish writing, which encapsulated a powerful idea so economically and elegantly. His fine prose allowed Abraham Lincoln and other social campaigners nearly a century later to champion the promises it made.

It is the opening paragraphs of the Declaration of Independence that inform the popular conception, although this leads us to judge the whole by one small section of the text. However, the document in its entirety is a masterful piece of prose, beautifully structured to great rhetorical effect. It also is a radical text, justifying the right to overthrow a government once it no longer represents the will of the people. The story of its composition, as much as its famous content, reflects the turmoil and excitement of the birth of a nation. The ongoing process of interpretation and reinterpretation since the revolutionary period illustrates how the document is at the heart of America's continuous quest to live up to its founding ideals.

UNDERSTANDING THE DECLARATION OF INDEPENDENCE
CONTEXT AND CREATORS

[W]e have every opportunity and every encouragement before us, to form the noblest, purest constitution on the face of the earth. We have it in our power to begin the world over again . . . The birth-day of a new world is at hand, and a race of men perhaps as numerous as all Europe contains, are to receive their portion of freedom from the events of a few months.

Thomas Paine, *Common Sense*, 1776

At the close of the French and Indian Wars (the Seven Years War) in 1763, the British Empire was transformed. The Peace of Paris, which ended the war, dramatically increased British possessions internationally—not only did Britain take control of the bulk of North America, winning Canada from the French, but eastern India also fell under its sway. The 13 American colonies were no longer Britain's flagship foreign territory, but represented instead just a small proportion of its colonial possessions.

Victory in the French and Indian Wars left the American colonists feeling confident and independent. The threats to their western borders, both from the French and from the Native Americans, were settled and so the colonists felt less dependent on the British for military support. At the same time, the British Parliament faced a pressing need to organize and administer its newly vast empire—and in a cost-effective fashion.

Until this point the British had kept a loose rein on the American colonies. Each of the 13 colonies was

Celebrations mark the Peace of Paris, signed in 1763 and bringing the French and Indian Wars to a close. The treaty's conditions were very favorable to British interests, particularly in North America.

nominally run by a colonial governor, appointed by the crown but paid for by the colonial assemblies (except in the case of Georgia, where the crown paid the governor's retainer). Although the governor had extensive powers, including the right to veto any measures passed by the colonial assemblies and even the ability to call for the dissolution of the assemblies, these powers were rarely, if ever, applied. The governors answered to the British government, which was not greatly concerned with the colonies, except insofar as they contributed to British trade and commerce, and rarely ordered any action. As a result, the colonies effectively had home rule.

The war had been expensive, leaving Britain with a national debt topping £130 million, and British taxpayers, already taxed at 20 percent, were unwilling to bear an additional tax burden. At the same time, the cost of administering the American colonies as they stood, including maintaining a standing army for the defense of its western borders, was not inconsiderable—in 1764 it topped £350,000. So the need to raise revenue was pressing, and to Parliament it seemed clear that the colonies would have to start paying for themselves.

However, for all that Parliament had clear ambitions, it had to contend with a young king. George III acceded to the British throne in 1760, when he was just 22 years old. Although he was raised to be king, he was still inexperienced and idealistic. He had an uneasy relationship with Parliament in the early years of his reign, and the first ten years saw a rapid succession of prime ministers, resulting in governmental instability. It was not until 1770 that George III was to find a prime minister—Lord North—with whom he could work peacefully.

Such instability was detrimental to the American colonies, for although the colonists persistently addressed the king in their circulars and petitions, it was Parliament that controlled the purse strings, levying taxes and setting colonial policy. This was a fact recognized by Benjamin Franklin, who was in London from 1764 and tried valiantly to influence Parliamentary policy in favor of the American colonies, tirelessly lobbying members of Parliament and influential private citizens.

The Sugar Act

The first attempt by Parliament to raise revenue from the colonies was the Revenue Act of 1764, commonly known as the Sugar Act. The text of the act said that the revenue raised would go toward defraying the cost of colonial administration. It reduced the duty on foreign molasses by 50 percent, but also levied duties on the importation of European luxury goods into the colonies, such as linen, silk, and wine. In addition it restricted U.S. exports of certain products, such as fur and hides, making England the sole market.

Fearful of the effects on their economies, and resentful of the increased duties, eight of the 13 colonies penned respectful petitions to the king against the Sugar Act.

WILLIAM JACKSON,

an *IMPORTER*;

It is defired that the Sons and Daughters of *LIBERTY,* would not buy any one thing of him, for in fo doing they will bring Difgrace upon *themfelves,* and their *Pofterity,* for *ever* and *ever,* AMEN.

Angered by what they considered excessive taxation, the colonists organized various non-importation movements, boycotting English goods and refusing to do business with those merchants who continued to trade in British products.

The act also inspired local protests, such as boycotts on the imported products newly attracting higher rates of duty. This was the birth of the non-importation movement. Although in its early days it had little effect on the British economy, it later played a greater role in asserting colonial power and independence.

In this cartoon the British prime minister, George Grenville, carries the Stamp Act of 1765 to a tomb where other unpopular laws already lie buried. The act was repealed after only one year, when mob violence against British agents made it impossible to enforce it.

The Stamp Act

Despite American dissatisfaction with the increased duties, Parliament persisted in its attempts to raise revenue from America, passing the Stamp Act of 1765, one of the last acts of the ministry of George Grenville (1763–65). Under the terms of the first direct tax to be levied on the colonies, revenue stamps, purchased from American agents appointed by the crown, were to be affixed to all printed matter, from newspapers and pamphlets to licenses and legal documents.

The fury inspired in the colonies by this act astonished the British. Organized groups of colonial businessmen, known as Sons of Liberty, fought back. Stamp agents were attacked and their stamps destroyed; mobs assaulted British officials and looted their homes and offices. The non-importation movement gained pace. In the summer after the passage of the act, trade with Britain fell by around £300,000. However, within the colonies business continued as normal—without stamps.

Protest was not limited to the grassroots level. Throughout the colonies, state assemblies met and declared the Stamp Act contrary to their state charters or constitutions. On Massachusetts's instigation, representatives from nine of the 13 colonies gathered in New York in October for what became known as the Stamp Act Congress. The Congress passed resolutions declaring that Parliament had no right to levy taxes on the colonies—"no taxation without representation." Although continuing to pledge loyalty to the crown, the Americans were standing up for their rights and showing a united front. The Stamp Act Congress was not the first time that the various colonial assemblies tried to work together—in 1754 the Albany Congress had been convened to devise a unified plan for defense against the Native Americans and the French who were threatening the colonies' western borders—but it was the first time that they were able to agree on policy.

The Stamp Act proved to be unenforceable, because of mob violence rather than the official protest of the Congress. It was repealed by Parliament in March 1766 by the short-lived ministry of Lord Rockingham (1765–66), with the king's support. Celebrations took place as soon as the news reached the colonies, honoring the king and expressing continued loyalty to the crown.

Although the Americans had won a victory of sorts, and Parliament had been forced to give way, the Declaratory Act was passed the same day as the repeal. This act stressed Parliament's rights over the colonies "in all cases whatsoever." Yet the Americans celebrated their victory, ignoring the ominous words of the Declaratory Act. They had

seen that Parliament would bend to their united will and had discovered a new confidence and political awareness throughout the colonies.

The Townshend Acts

Parliament had not abandoned its plan to raise revenue from the colonies. Under the ministry of Lord Chatham (1766–68), it followed quickly with the Townshend Acts of 1767. Lowering British land taxes to 15 percent (from 20 percent), it raised customs duties in America on imported British necessities such as glass, tea, paper, paint, and lead. This was not a direct tax, but rather additional import duties of the kind Britain had always levied. To enforce collection of the new duties, Parliament reorganized the customs service and created a new civil service, with its salaries to be paid by the crown, not the local assemblies. Crucially, it also undertook to pay the salaries of the colonial governors, making them independent of local control. On top of all this, the British army was pulled back from the western borders, where it had been stationed to prevent Native American (and French) attacks, and was relocated in the more populous, coastal regions—placing a standing army among the American citizenry.

Again the Americans fought back. Highly effective importation boycotts cut British imports by two-thirds. Sons of Liberty throughout the colonies organized protests, and Daughters of Liberty held spinning bees at which they wove sufficient homespun to clothe their communities.

The British government used military force to control riots protesting the Townshend Acts. Five colonists died during the "Boston Massacre" on March 5, 1770, shot by British Redcoats, as shown in this 1770 etching.

This time the British authorities were not prepared to tolerate protest or disobedience. The new ministry of Frederick, Lord North (1770–82) was determined to follow a path of non-conciliation with the American colonies. So after the Massachusetts House of Representatives passed a circular letter to the other colonial assemblies, calling for a respectful joint petition to the king, Parliament ordered the governor to dismiss the assembly if it did not retract the circular. This was a bold command, doomed to failure. In making the order, Parliament must have been aware that it was risking blatant refusal from the Massachusetts House of Representatives. After refusing to retract by a majority of 92 to 17, the assembly was dissolved by the crown, and violent protests broke out throughout the colony. Similar violence erupted in New York.

To restore peace, the British government resorted to military force, stationing around 4,000 soldiers in Boston and similar numbers in New York. Tensions ran high, particularly after one civilian death in the Gordon Hill riot in New York and five more in the "Boston Massacre" on March 5, 1770. The British government had lost control over the colonies.

As with its other attempts to generate revenue in the colonies, the Townshend Acts were deemed to be a failure and were repealed by Parliament on the very day of the Boston Massacre. Ironically, only the new duty on tea was retained, a token gesture by Parliament to save face. But tea was very soon to become the focus of growing American radicalism.

"The die is cast"

When the East India Company was granted a monopoly on the import of tea to the colonies, Americans fought back again. Non-importation protests saw the imported tea boycotted and returned to England unsold. In Boston, Samuel Adams devised an ingenious protest display: on the night of December 16, 1773, Sons of Liberty in disguise as Native American warriors boarded three British ships and dumped their loads of tea leaves into the water. This blatant display of disrespect inflamed British sentiment as much as it delighted radical Americans.

"The die is cast," wrote George III when news of the Boston Tea Party reached him. "The colonies must either submit or triumph."

Parliament responded with the Coercive Acts of 1774—known by the colonists as the Intolerable Acts. Hoping to isolate Massachusetts, Parliament closed its port until the tea was paid for, altered the system of government in the colony to give Britain direct rule, and allowed the confiscation of American property to provide shelter and supplies for the British army. At the same time, the Quebec Act of 1774 defined the border of Quebec at the Appalachian Mountains, limiting westward expansion.

The Continental Congresses

In response to the Coercive Acts and the threat to Massachusetts's autonomy, the Virginia Assembly called for a congress to be attended by representatives of all 13

The Boston Tea Party, organized by Samuel Adams, protested against the monopoly on tea granted to the East India Company. The boldness and theatricality of the protest inspired many American patriots, and the audacious challenge to British authority meant that there was no turning back from war.

Delegates to the First Continental Congress in 1774 met in Carpenter's Hall in Philadelphia, Pennsylvania. The aim was to reach a peaceful settlement with the British government, improving relations and releasing the colonies from restrictive measures.

American colonies. The First Continental Congress met in Philadelphia on September 12, with 12 of the 13 colonies attending (only Georgia was absent).

Congress's desire was not for independence from Britain; rather, it aimed for self-rule within the British Empire. Because the American colonies were not represented in Parliament—and both sides recognized that physical distance made direct representation impossible—the Americans believed that Parliament had no right to legislate for the colonies. Britain asserted its sovereignty over the colonies by stressing that they were "virtually" represented, in the same way as the majority of the population of Britain was—only a small minority of the British people had the right to vote, yet elected officials legislated for all of them.

The Continental Congress hoped to restore peaceful relations with Britain, putting just enough pressure on the mother country to encourage Parliament to withdraw its restrictive measures, but not so much as to worsen relations between the two. It issued a statement, titled the "Declaration of Rights and Grievances," which it addressed to the people of Great Britain, and a petition to King George III; both accepted Parliament's regulation of American commerce, but rejected any further legislation. The Congress also agreed upon an "Association"—basically a series of graduating economic embargoes on British imports and American exports to Britain, as well as an infrastructure to enforce them. If these measures failed to achieve any progress, then a second Congress would be called in the spring of 1775.

In contrast to these moderate statements, the Congress also endorsed the Suffolk Resolves, a statement penned by Massachusetts assemblies that rejected the Coercive Acts as contrary to their state charters or constitutions, and called upon the people of the colony to rise against the British occupation. This radical statement was tantamount to a declaration of war against Great Britain.

At the time John Adams, a delegate from Massachusetts, had little hope that Congress's actions would be effective. He wrote in a later memoir:

> When congress had finished their business, as they thought, in the autumn of 1774, I had with Mr. [Patrick] Henry, before we took leave of each other, some familiar conversation, in which I expressed a full conviction that our resolves, declaration of rights, enumeration of wrongs, petitions, remonstrances, and addresses, associations and non-importation agreements, however they might be viewed in America, and however necessary to cement the union of the colonies, would be but waste water in England.

And he was not wrong.

Parliament's response to Congress's petitions was moderate, but hardly far-reaching enough to satisfy American wishes for self-rule. The North Conciliatory Resolve offered that any colony that could fund its own government, plus pay a contribution (to be determined by Britain) for its defense,

The petition issued by the First Continental Congress to King George III accepted Parliament's regulation of American commerce, but did not recognize Parliament's right to legislate for the colonies over any other issues.

The first shot in the American Revolution was fired at Lexington, Massachusetts (top). British soldiers were en route to Concord to confiscate arms collected by American rebels, when Paul Revere (above, in a 1768 portrait by John Singleton Copley) spread the word of the British maneuvers, warning the patriots so they could organize their own defense. Revere was an active member of the Sons of Liberty and one of New England's finest silversmiths.

would not be taxed by Britain; in addition any local customs duties would be paid into the colony's own treasury. But it did not revoke the sanctions placed on Massachusetts—and at any rate, events in Massachusetts would make all attempts at compromise futile.

General Thomas Gage, the British military leader who was also the appointed governor of Massachusetts, was ordered to enforce the Coercive Acts and arrest rebel leaders. On April 18, 1775, he sent a division of his garrison to confiscate arms being gathered by rebels in Concord, outside Boston, but the news was spread in advance by Paul Revere and other patriots, allowing the colonists to gather and arm for their defense. The first shot was fired in Lexington, en route to Concord—nobody knows who pulled the trigger.

The Second Continental Congress convened on May 10, 1775, as planned, with John Hancock, a wealthy businessman from Boston, chosen as president. War had already begun, and the Congress became effectively the central government for the united colonies. It formed an army under the leadership of George Washington, set up a committee to approach foreign countries with a view to forming alliances and attracting financial aid, and organized funding for its war effort.

Within a year, the members of this Congress would achieve lasting fame as the signatories of the Declaration of Independence. Yet at this point the Congress was still not calling for independence, but for reconciliation. It issued a "Declaration of the Causes and Necessity of Taking Up

Arms," written by John Dickinson of Pennsylvania and Thomas Jefferson, in which Congress asserted that "We mean not to dissolve that union which has so long and so happily subsisted between us. Necessity has not yet driven us into that desperate measure, or induced us to excite any other nation to war against them."

Dickinson had also written the "Declaration of Rights and Grievances" issued earlier by the Stamp Act Congress, but he was best known as the author of "Letters from a Farmer in Pennsylvania to the Inhabitants of the British Colonies," which were published in numerous colonial newspapers around the time of the Townshend Acts. Their moderate point of view helped win over many conservative colonists to the patriot cause. Later Dickinson would refuse to sign the Declaration of Independence, still hoping against hope for reconciliation.

At the same time as it was preparing for war, Congress tried once more to calm the situation, issuing the "Olive Branch Petition" to George III in July 1775, on Dickinson's urging. The petition was signed by nearly all the men who would put their names to the Declaration of Independence just one year later. It was the result of an internal compromise. By this point, the majority of Congress was in favor of independence, and that majority agreed to dispatch the petition, hoping that, were it rejected, the members still opposed to independence would be swayed.

When the petition reached London, George III was no longer in a mood for compromise and refused even to take

The title page from the first printing of Thomas Paine's *Common Sense*. The pamphlet made the case for independence in plain language and was hugely influential in winning support for the cause of American independence.

delivery of it. In August 1775 he declared that the colonies were in a state of rebellion, and the British military response began in earnest, countered by organized American forces.

Common Sense

In January 1776 came the publication of Thomas Paine's *Common Sense*, a political pamphlet that made explicit the as-yet-unspoken case for independence. It went through 25 printings in its first year alone, selling more than 150,000 copies in its first few weeks, and was read by nearly every man in the colonies.

Paine, a Quaker, had emigrated from England to America in 1774. He had met and impressed Benjamin Franklin while in London, and Franklin had given him several letters of introduction to use in America. A self-educated journalist, Paine wrote with passion, using language accessible to the ordinary man, rather than the more scholarly and complex prose normally used by pamphleteers. His style was not unlike Franklin's, and many people initially suspected that Franklin was the author of *Common Sense*, since at the time of publication Paine was unknown.

In bold terms, Paine attacked the monarchy: not just the concept of it, but also George III himself, whom he referred to as "the royal brute of Great Britain." He maintained that monarchy, by vesting so much control in an individual, was unnatural and prone to corruption: as he wrote, "Of more worth is one honest man to society and in the sight of God, than all the crowned ruffians that ever

Thomas Paine arrived in America from Britain in 1774. Throughout the American Revolution, his pamphlets drummed up enthusiasm for the patriot cause. Afterward, he returned to London, where he was convicted of treason in 1792 for his political writings.

lived." Hereditary rule meant that leaders were far removed from the common people over whom they governed. Hopes for reconciliation were "a fallacious dream," with Paine proposing instead a system of representative government for the colonies that was broadly similar to what was already in place. In his view the choice was simple—either remaining under a tyrant in an inequitable system, or gaining freedom and prosperity.

Representatives to the Congress sent copies of *Common Sense* back home to help win support from their constituents. Although his ideas were not new, Paine summarized contemporary thinking in an eloquent and persuasive manner, which helped to sway the will of the population in favor of independence.

Independence

Events moved quickly in the first five months of 1776. In March, North Carolina's assembly became the first to vote in favor of independence. Congress passed the Privateering Resolution, establishing a navy, and in April it opened the American ports to commercial ships from other nations, breaking British control over its commerce once and for all. At the beginning of May, John Adams proposed that Congress advise each colony to establish an independent state government. This resolution was adopted: "That it be recommended to all the colonies, which had not already established governments suited to the exigencies of their case, to adopt such governments as would, in the opinion of the representatives of the people, best conduce to the happiness and safety of their constituents in particular, and Americans in general." That same month, Congress learned that Britain had hired German mercenaries to fight against the colonists, thereby bringing foreign involvement to the conflict.

On June 7, 1776, Richard Henry Lee, a delegate from Virginia, proposed to Congress the following motion: "That these United Colonies are, and of right ought to be, Free and Independent States, and that they are absolved from all allegiance to the British crown, and that all political connection between them and the State of Great Britain is, and ought to be, totally dissolved."

Because Virginia was not only the most populous, but also the wealthiest, of the American colonies, this statement carried extra weight by virtue of being delivered by a Virginia delegate. The Virginia House of Burgesses (as the assembly there was known) had made the decision in May that it would send a delegate to the Congress to propose independence.

A member of the Virginia Sons of Liberty, Lee was long active in the Virginia legislature in favor of American liberty, along with Thomas Jefferson and Patrick Henry. He was the most vocal of Virginia's delegates to the Continental Congresses; in fact, many considered him one of the best speakers in America (he was more than once compared to Cicero). Although it was customary for the proposer of a motion to be given the honor of chairing the committee that

would write it up, Lee was not appointed to the committee to compose the Declaration of Independence; instead Jefferson represented Virginia on the committee. At the time, it was said that Lee withdrew because his wife's illness necessitated his return home, but it is more likely that he was considered too radical—and had made too many enemies in Congress—to handle such a delicate job. However, he was one of the signers and later played a key role in getting the Bill of Rights—the first ten amendments to the Constitution—passed by Congress.

Richard Henry Lee, long a committed patriot, was the delegate to the Continental Congress from the Virginia House of Burgesses. Noted for his eloquence, he gave the speech that introduced the motion calling for independence for the American colonies.

The passion of Lee's closing words gives a clear picture of his famed eloquence:

Why then, sir, why do we longer delay? Why still deliberate? Let this happy day give birth to an American republic. Let her arise, not to devastate and to conquer, but to re-establish the reign of peace and of law. The eyes of Europe are fixed upon us: she demands of us a living example of freedom, that may exhibit a contrast in the felicity of the citizen to the ever increasing tyranny which desolates her polluted shores. She invites us to prepare an asylum, where the unhappy may find solace, and the persecuted repose. She entreats us to cultivate a propitious soil, where the generous plant which first sprung and grew in England, but is now withered by the poisonous blasts of Scottish tyranny, may revive and flourish, sheltering under its salubrious and interminable shade, all the unfortunate of the human race. If we are not this day wanting in our

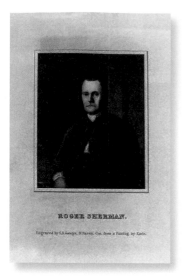

ROGER SHERMAN.

Engraved by S.S.Jocelyn, N Haven, Con. from a Painting by Earle.

Roger Sherman, delegate to the Continental Congress from Connecticut, was a member of the drafting committee. He was the only man to sign not only the Declaration of Independence but also the Articles of Association, the Articles of Confederation, and the Constitution.

duty, the names of the American legislators of 1776 will be placed by posterity at the side of Theseus, Lycurgus, and Romulus, of the three Williams of Nassau, and of all those whose memory has been, and ever will be, dear to virtuous men and good citizens.

The heated debate that followed lasted two days, and the vote was delayed for three weeks, in order for representatives from those states that had not yet approved the vote for independence—namely Maryland, Delaware, New Jersey, and New York—to return home to win support for the motion.

Yet at the same time as it postponed the vote, Congress (optimistic that the vote would ultimately be successful) established a committee to prepare its Declaration of Independence. The committee's five members were as follows: Benjamin Franklin of Pennsylvania, John Adams of Massachusetts, Roger Sherman of Connecticut, Robert R. Livingston of New York, and Thomas Jefferson of Virginia.

Although these men were entrusted to this important task, it was by no means the limit of their responsibilities. Adams and Franklin were also involved in preparing treaties to submit to foreign powers; Adams was on the Board of War; Livingston and Sherman were on the committee that was preparing articles of confederation; and Jefferson himself was on several committees concentrating on relations with Canada, as well as one that drew up rules for congressional debates.

Roger Sherman was already prominent in local politics when he was selected to represent his home state of Connecticut in both Continental Congresses. He was on the committee with Adams to establish a Board of War to administer the army, and on another committee, with Jefferson, to investigate a misconduct in Canada; and with Robert Livingston he was on the committee to draft the Articles of Confederation. Although he seems to have contributed relatively little to the actual composition of the Declaration, he was noted for his common sense, fairness, and integrity, and he must have been a stabilizing influence on all the groups with whom he worked. Sherman later served as a member of the Constitutional Convention and was a staunch supporter of the new Constitution. He also served both as a member of the House of Representatives and as a senator.

Robert R. Livingston never signed the Declaration of Independence, even though he was on the drafting committee, because he did not receive authorization to do so from the New York provincial congress. He came from a family that had long held political influence in New York. His grandfather, who had emigrated from Scotland, was one of the wealthiest men in the state, through the combination of a clever marriage and trade with Native Americans. He was secretary of Indian affairs for more than 30 years and was also a member of the state assembly. Livingston's father was a Whig political leader, serving as a state judge and as a delegate to the Stamp Congress. Livingston himself trained as a lawyer and was a

Robert R. Livingston, the delegate from New York, was part of an American family that was prominent during the colonial and post-colonial periods. Although he was a member of the drafting committee, he did not sign the Declaration of Independence.

Benjamin Franklin in 1785 on his return from France after negotiating the Treaty of Paris. He was one of America's leading statesmen in the revolutionary period, yet even his strenuous efforts and diplomacy could not prevent the war. As a member of the drafting committee, he made only a few changes to Jefferson's draft, but they proved to be significant ones.

partner of John Jay, who was later to negotiate the Treaty of Paris with Great Britain at the end of the war. Livingston, as the first secretary of the department of foreign affairs, issued the instructions to the diplomats—including Jay. Later he served as minister to France under Thomas Jefferson, where he negotiated the terms of the Louisiana Purchase.

Benjamin Franklin was the elder statesman of the group. Unwell at the time, suffering from gout and boils on his leg, he played little part in creating the first draft of the Declaration of Independence, but made some minor yet crucial changes before Jefferson submitted the document to Congress as a whole. Later on, Franklin expressed no regret at missing a chance to be credited as the author of so historic a document: "I have made it a rule, whenever in my power, to avoid becoming the draughtsman of papers to be reviewed by a public body." Thomas Jefferson, who was much aggrieved by the substantial editing that Congress imposed on his draft, surely sympathized with this position.

Franklin was a slow convert to the idea of independence. Born in Boston, he moved to Philadelphia as a young man and came to public attention as the publisher of the *Pennsylvania Gazette* newspaper. A true polymath, Franklin made as many contributions to science—such as his invention of bifocals and lightning rods—as he did to public life. He spent 18 years in England, trying to lobby Parliament to act favorably not only toward his home state of Pennsylvania, but also in relation to all the American colonies, and in fact considered during that period making London his home.

A supporter of the British Empire, Franklin saw benefits to the whole of America remaining part of it. He recognized that one day America would be stronger in terms of both its numbers and its resources than the mother country and hoped for a union of equal benefit to both parties. As late as January 1775, Franklin was sitting in the gallery of the House of Lords, advocating a moderate proposal to offer limited autonomy to the colonies. But he returned to America later that year, aged 69, when it became clear to him that the rift between crown and colonies was irreparable, and he was a dedicated convert to the cause of independence. Late in 1776 he returned to Europe as the preeminent American diplomat, seeking support from France and later starting negotiations for the peace settlement with Britain.

John Adams—ambitious, outspoken, and frank, both in his speeches and in his writing—came to prominence in Massachusetts, that hotbed of radicalism, as an opponent of the Stamp Act and was a longtime supporter of independence. As early as 1755 he wrote the following:

> Soon after the reformation, a few people came over into this new world for conscience sake: perhaps this apparently trivial incident may transfer the great seat of empire into America. It looks likely to me; for, if we can remove the turbulent Gallicks, our people according to the exactest [sic] computations, will in another century become more numerous than England

JOHN ADAMS,
2ND PRESIDENT OF THE UNITED STATES.
PHILADELPHIA.

John Adams was known to be fiery and opinionated, but few politicians were more dedicated to the cause of American independence. His membership in the drafting committee was the start of a lifelong rivalry with Thomas Jefferson—Adams resented the way Jefferson's contributions were celebrated in the years that followed.

itself. Should this be the case, since we have, I may say, all the naval shores of the nation in our hands, it will be easy to obtain a mastery of the seas; and the united force of all Europe will not be able to subdue us. The only way to keep us from setting up for ourselves is to disunite us.

In his autobiography, written in 1805, Adams claimed that the committee appointed both him and Jefferson to the task of drawing up the Declaration, but that he regretfully declined the honor, for a number of reasons, including the fact that he "had a great Opinion of the Elegance of his [Jefferson's] pen and none at all of my own." Jefferson contested this version of events, claiming that he alone was selected by the committee, but that he did submit an early draft to both Adams and Franklin and that, like Franklin, Adams made few changes.

This statue of Thomas Jefferson stands under the domed rotunda of the Jefferson Memorial in Washington, D.C. On the walls around the statue are Jefferson's words from the Declaration of Independence.

Although Adams played little role in the composition of the Declaration of Independence, he was one of its strongest supporters, speaking out persuasively on many different occasions. In 1777 he sailed to France to become a member of America's team of diplomats, but his outspoken nature meant that he was not best suited to this job. Nonetheless, he remained in this role off and on until 1788, helping to negotiate the Treaty of Paris in September 1783, returning to become George Washington's vice president and later the second president of the United States.

Today Thomas Jefferson is famous as the author of the Declaration of Independence—and as the third president of the United States—and we ascribe to him the majesty that such responsibilities entail. To his contemporaries, Jefferson was a shy, aloof character, although everyone accepted that he was keenly intelligent and extraordinarily well read. Tall and gangly, with red hair, Jefferson was a poor public speaker in an age when fine oratory was well respected. He was described thus in middle age, after his appointment as first secretary of state: "His whole figure has a loose, shackling air. He had a rambling vacant look, and nothing of that firm collected deportment . . . even his discourse partook of his personal demeanor. It was loose and rambling, and yet he scattered information wherever he went, and some even brilliant sentiments sparkled from him."

Jefferson was the son of a wealthy landowner, but a self-made one, who earned his living as a surveyor. His mother, however, came from one of Virginia's leading families. A keen student, Jefferson studied classics as a young man and then law at William & Mary College. Although he was a poor speaker, he was an excellent scholar with a retentive memory. After a short and undistinguished career as a lawyer, he entered the Virginia House of Burgesses in 1768, just as the debate over taxation was gaining pace. Jefferson was unwavering in his support for American rights, and his positions were ably put in his pamphlet "A Summary View of the Rights of British America," which was published by the Continental Congress without his consent in 1774.

Thomas Jefferson designed his own home, Monticello, near Charlottesville, Virginia. Building work began in 1770, and in 1772 Jefferson moved in, although he continued to alter and add to the house for years afterward. It is a prime example of the American classical revival style.

In this document he stressed that loyalty to the king was purely voluntary, and he rejected Parliamentary authority in the colonies.

Jefferson was a reluctant entrant to national politics, focusing instead on Virginia. He did not serve in the First Continental Congress, and was a delegate to the Second Continental Congress only as a substitute for Peyton Randolph, who was required in the Virginia House of Burgesses.

He was quick to get back to his home state. In October 1776 he returned to Virginia to put his principles into practice. He campaigned for the abolition of primogeniture and entail, ending the hereditary aristocracy (from which he himself benefited), and for the separation of church and state and religious freedom. His term as governor of Virginia (1779–81) was a difficult time, as he presided over the last years of the American Revolution, when the American forces were depleted in funds as well as energy. He returned to the service of the nation as a delegate to the Continental Congress (1783–84); as ambassador to France, succeeding Benjamin Franklin in 1785; and then as secretary of state and vice president.

Thomas Jefferson's political career culminated in two terms as president (1801–09), and he was the first president to be inaugurated in Washington, D.C. As president, he was a staunch advocate of states' rights, believing that the role of the federal government was largely restricted to foreign affairs. A believer in the power of the written word, he also believed in the literal interpretation of the Constitution, as opposed to those who promoted the idea of "implied powers."

After his presidency Jefferson retired happily to Monticello, his home in Virginia, which he designed himself. He devoted himself to his writing and his scholarship, and also founded the University of Virginia. Today the achievements of his long career are celebrated by the Jefferson Memorial in Washington, D.C., as well as in countless libraries and archives.

UNDERSTANDING THE DECLARATION OF INDEPENDENCE
THE DOCUMENT

When forced, therefore, to resort to arms for redress, an appeal to the tribunal of the world was deemed proper for our justification. This was the object of the Declaration of Independence. Not to find out new principles, or new arguments, never before thought of, not merely to say things which had never been said before; but to place before mankind the common sense of the subject, in terms so plain and firm as to command their assent, and to justify ourselves in the independent stand we are compelled to take. Neither aiming at originality of principle or sentiment, nor yet copied from any particular and previous writing, it was intended to be an expression of the American mind, and to give to that expression the proper tone and spirit called for by the occasion.

Thomas Jefferson to Henry Lee, 1825 (Jefferson, *Writings*, 1984)

As Thomas Jefferson was composing the Declaration of Independence, he was open to many different influences. Throughout his life he was an avid scholar and widely read, familiar not just with contemporary authors, such as the English philosophers John Locke and Algernon Sidney, but also with the classics.

Jefferson was equally aware of other important historical documents of the time, and he had even played a role in writing some of them, such as the Virginia Constitution. All of these various influences are quite evident in his work.

Yet the fact that echoes of these sources are apparent in the Declaration of Independence in no way detracts from its quality. Jefferson himself made no great claim to originality. As he later wrote, "All its authority rests then on the harmonizing sentiments of the day, whether expressed in conversation, in letters, printed essays, or in the elementary books of public right, as Aristotle, Cicero, Locke, Sidney &c." In fact, in Jefferson's time the ability to borrow, to use references to other works and authors, was an indication of learnedness that was as prized and respected as originality is today.

Top: the Enlightenment philosopher John Locke was one of Jefferson's inspirations.

Above: Algernon Sidney was one of the most influential political theorists in the seventeenth century. His advocacy of questioning authority and overthrowing governments that did not suit the needs of the people found many adherents throughout the American colonies.

The Philosophical Current

Although today virtually unknown, Algernon Sidney (1622–83) was one of the most influential political theorists of the seventeenth and eighteenth centuries, and many of his ideas underlie the positions taken by the major Enlightenment philosophers who followed him, including the leading American politicians.

Sidney, the second son of the 2nd Earl of Leicester, fought with the Parliamentarians during the English Civil War and served in the Long Parliament, but was opposed to Oliver Cromwell's tendency toward dictatorialism. He was abroad at the time of the Restoration, and after his return to England he associated with the opponents of Charles II and negotiated with the French and Dutch to win their support for a rebellion against the king. After Charles II suspended Parliament, some of his opponents feared that he was aiming

As he was composing the Declaration of Independence, Thomas Jefferson lived in lodgings in Graff House in Philadelphia. Today the building, known as Declaration House, is part of the Independence National Historic Park.

to return to an absolute monarchy, and they formed a conspiracy to assassinate him, which became known as the Rye House Plot. Although Sidney was probably not involved, his other activities against the king came to light, and he was charged with treason. The evidence against him was wholly circumstantial, based largely on his writings, the unpublished "Discourses Concerning Government" (1689); nonetheless he was found guilty and beheaded.

Sidney and his work were well respected in the American colonies. He was a contemporary and friend of William Penn, the founder of Pennsylvania, and he supported the founding ideals of liberty and religious freedom. Later his work was cited by John Adams, Benjamin Franklin, Samuel Adams, and James Madison. In his founding essays for the University of Virginia, Thomas Jefferson ranked Sidney's ideas with Locke's in terms of their influence in America.

In Sidney's view, liberty—the freedom to pursue happiness and financial well-being—was a God-given right (bear in mind that he was writing before the secularizing effects of the Enlightenment; later this concept would be put in terms of natural law). Laws, constructed by man, exist only to protect and preserve liberty. He wrote, "[I]f the safety of the people be the supreme law, and this safety extend to, and consist in, the preservation of their liberties, goods, lands, and lives, that law must necessarily be the root and the beginning, as well as the end and the limit, of all magistratical power, and all laws must be subservient and subordinate to it."

It was not the form of government that determined whether it was bad or good; rather, each government should be judged on its aims and achievements. Sidney was not an opponent of monarchy, although he found that monarchies were more prone to corruption and misrule than republican governments. As he wrote, "The difference between good governments and ill governments is not that those of one sort have an arbitrary power which the others have not, for they all have it; but that those which are well constituted, place this power so as it may be beneficial to the people, and set such rules as are hardly to be transgressed; whilst those of the other sort fail in one or both of these points." The idea that law should be easily obeyed suited the American people, who felt aggrieved by unsuitable regulations imposed by a distant government that was not aware of their particular situation.

Like the Enlightenment thinkers to whom he was an inspiration, Sidney advocated questioning authority. "Who will wear a shoe that hurts him, because the shoe-maker tells him 'tis well made? . . . Such as have reason, understanding, or common sense, will, and ought to make use of it in those things that concern themselves and their posterity." By taking a critical stance toward those who rule over them, people will be able to ensure that their government remains equitable.

If government is found to be lacking, then man, who has created and affirmed it, also has the right to dissolve it, in Sidney's view. His radical advocacy of revolution won many converts in the colonies, especially since any rebellion was only to follow rational examination. However, his was not a call for hotheaded insurrection, but for responsible representative government. "God leaves to Man the choice of Forms in Government, and those who constitute one Form, may abrogate it . . . The general revolt of a Nation cannot be called a Rebellion." For Sidney, force was a final recourse, for he maintained that a government that comes to power through force, and maintains its authority through force, is likely to be overturned by force—yet force may sometimes be necessary to implement a form of government that will win universal consent.

The Enlightenment
The political ferment in America was taking place in the context of the Enlightenment, the transforming intellectual movement that swept through Europe as well as the New World. The Declaration of Independence was inspired by the ideas of the Enlightenment—and also came to shape them. Jefferson and Franklin are considered key exponents of Enlightenment thought, and the Declaration of Independence one of its canonical texts.

A broad intellectual movement, the Enlightenment encompassed developments in science, philosophy, political theory, and theology. Enlightenment thinkers were committed to the idea of progress, and specifically progress through rational inquiry. Inspired by Isaac Newton's discoveries, which led to a great leap forward in understanding the

Isaac Newton's discoveries about the natural world inspired Enlightenment philosophers to extend the bounds of knowledge, investigating the way humans think and learn.

natural world, they sought to discover the universal principles—the natural laws, the clear, distinct, self-evident truths—that governed human existence.

British philosophers, such as John Locke and David Hume, were testing and expanding the bounds of human knowledge empirically, looking for the basis of knowledge in human sensation and experience. Locke's concept of the tabula rasa (that at birth each person is a "blank slate" on which family and society inscribe their wisdom and mores) was a key Enlightenment concept. For example, one of the reasons that the Encyclopedists in France produced their grand *Encyclopédie* was to share and disseminate knowledge, convinced as they were of the vast capacity for learning inherent in all of us.

These themes taken together—the basis of knowledge in sensation, and the tabula rasa—also implied the idea that all men are equal, at least at birth, and that only social advantages distinguish one from another. Despite any advantages accruing from social situation, all men are capable of sensation, and thus of learning from this sensation. In other words, knowledge is accessible to all. The tabula rasa concept was extremely influential in the American colonies, where radicals came to think of the New World as a vast blank slate, where the social order could be created anew.

Because in the Enlightenment scheme everything is subject to rational investigation, both church and state lost some of their mystique—they were no longer seen as unquestionable. Just as theologians revised their relationship to divinity, so did political thinkers alter their ideas about the relationship of government and the people. Many of these ideas are obvious in the prefatory paragraphs of the Declaration of Independence.

In a rational social order, so went the Enlightenment theory, government existed to protect the right of man to pursue his own goal, which was essentially happiness or well-being. Man is motivated by self-interest (his quest for happiness), and society/government is a social construct designed to protect each man, allowing all to live together in a mutually beneficial way.

Men create government to ensure their rights, and no legitimate government can exist without the consent of the governed; in other words, government is a social contract. The logical extension of this idea is that all men have the right to self-government, to a government of their own creation and their own choosing, to which they freely consent—and that, equally, they have the right of rebellion if the established government is no longer fulfilling its responsibilities.

The fact that Enlightenment thinking overwhelmingly rejected tyranny or other absolutist forms of government was a serious threat to established social orders around the world. Inspired by these ideas, the seventeenth and eighteenth centuries were a time of political upheaval, not only in America, but also in France, Russia, and the Spanish Empire, to name just a few.

Key Documents: The Declaration of Rights, 1689

In English politics, a declaration was a distinct type of document with a formal style, although not officially or legally defined. The special significance of statements made in the form of a declaration was understood by the government and the public alike. For the most part, declarations announced and implemented new policies. Because they were intended to win public support, they also usually included clear and persuasive explanatory passages. Throughout English history, declarations were issued both by Parliament and the monarch, and the American colonists were only following an accepted practice when they issued their own declarations—the Declaration on Taking Up Arms and the Declaration of Independence—to Britain.

In the colonies, the best known of the English declarations was the Declaration of Rights of 1689, the key text of the Glorious Revolution. This is the name given to a set of events surrounding James II's abdication of the throne. He fled without violence after arousing the enmity of the nation for his promotion of Roman Catholicism, despite Parliament's laws to the contrary. Upon the succession of William and Mary (Mary was James II's daughter), Parliament issued this Declaration. It was formally passed on December 16, 1689. After the coronation, two other key legislative acts followed: the Toleration Act, which mandated religious toleration; and the Triennial Act (1694), which provided for regular elections every three years and abolished the monarch's right to dissolve Parliament arbitrarily.

Top: **After James II's forces deserted him, he fled to France, as seen in this nineteenth-century pencil drawing.**

Above: **the Glorious Revolution was a bloodless coup that removed James II from the throne, replacing him with William and Mary, who ruled as joint sovereigns. This nineteenth-century oil painting shows James II receiving news of the landing of William of Orange, with his troops, in 1688.**

Thomas Jefferson would have seen the Virginia Declaration of Rights by the time he was composing the Declaration of Independence, and it clearly influenced his thinking and his phrasing.

The Declaration, also known as the Bill of Rights, was very popular in the American colonies. It consisted of three parts. First came an introductory passage that formally ended the reign of James II. A list of specific grievances against the king followed. It then moved on to a list of 13 "undoubted rights and liberties." It established limits on the monarch's legal rights, and protected Parliament's power to legislate—for example, reserving to Parliament the right to levy taxes. It also made the monarch subject to the laws of Parliament and abolished his power to change Parliament's laws arbitrarily. The list also included several rights asserted by the American colonists during their political struggle: the right of subjects to petition the king, and the right not to suffer a standing army during peacetime.

The Virginia Declaration of Rights

Two Virginia state documents mark a clear transition between the English Declaration of Rights and the Declaration of Independence: the Virginia Constitution, with its preamble written by Thomas Jefferson in the spring of 1776; and the Virginia Declaration of Rights, written by George Mason around the same time.

Each state was soon to adopt its own version of these documents, which established the basis for government in the state and defined fundamental liberties. Essentially the various parts of the English Declaration of Rights were reflected in the founding documents issued by each American state: declarations of independence, equating to the introductory paragraphs of the English declaration, were either issued individually by a state or sometimes incorporated into its constitution; a declaration (or bill) of rights, protecting individuals; and a constitution, establishing the parameters of government.

Jefferson used the English document as a model for the structure and sometimes the phrasing of the Virginia Constitution, which functioned as a break with the monarchy and a consequent establishment of a new government, for which the constitution was the defining document. He began, as in the earlier text, with a long "whereas" clause that establishes the subject of the grievances to follow: "Whereas George Guelf king of Great Britain and Ireland and Elector of Hanover, heretofore entrusted with the exercise of the kingly office in this government hath endeavored to pervert the same into a detestable and insupportable tyranny . . ."

After listing 16 specific grievances against the king, the final document, as edited by the Virginia Constitutional Convention, goes on to affirm that "the government of this country, as formerly exercised under the Crown of Great Britain, is totally dissolved."

The draft of the Virginia Declaration of Rights was available to Thomas Jefferson at the time the Declaration of Independence was composed, and exercised a clear influence. It was written by George Mason, whom Thomas Jefferson referred to as "the wisest man of his generation."

A Virginia plantation owner and near neighbor of George Washington, Mason became a convert to the idea of

The Virginia planter, George Mason, was a reluctant politician, but was convinced by his neighbor, George Washington, to take his seat in the Virginia House of Burgesses while the general was away with the Continental Army. The Virginia Declaration of Rights, which he wrote, proved to be one of the most influential early American documents, and its phrasing was echoed in many state constitutions.

freedom because of his dislike of excessive taxation. He was not interested in political office, but was persuaded by the gravity of events to assume Washington's seat in the Virginia House of Burgesses between 1775 and 1780 (when Washington was away with the Continental Army). It was then that he wrote, basically single-handedly, the state's Declaration of Rights, in which he expressed his belief in fundamental individual rights as well as in limited government. Later he became a member of the Constitutional Convention, but he refused to sign the Constitution because it lacked a Bill of Rights. His concerted advocacy of a Bill of Rights contributed to the adoption soon afterward of the first 10 amendments.

The Virginia Declaration begins with assertions that are echoed in the Declaration of Independence, albeit in Jefferson's (and Congress's) more elegant turn of phrase: "that all men are born equally free and independent, and have certain inherent natural rights, of which they cannot, by any compact, deprive or divert their posterity; among which are the enjoyment of life and liberty, with the means of acquiring and possessing property, and pursuing and obtaining happiness and safety."

The power of these sentiments must surely have reverberated with Thomas Jefferson as he was working on the Declaration of Independence. They also appear in the constitutions of many other states, and in fact even their phrasing was widely imitated, rather than Thomas Jefferson's more artful phrasing.

"An expression of the American mind"

Thomas Jefferson penned the Declaration in very short order. As John Adams recalled, "We were all in haste; Congress was impatient." Nothing is known of Jefferson's creative process; he once wrote that he made no claims to originality, but rather intended the text to be "an expression of the American mind." It is easier to trace what happened to the text once Jefferson issued it to the drafting committee and then to Congress.

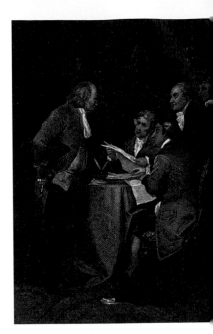

This engraving shows the drafting committee at work: Benjamin Franklin, Thomas Jefferson, John Adams, Robert Livingston, and Roger Sherman. Little is known about the activities of the committee since no minutes of their meetings were kept.

The drafting committee was established by Congress only on June 11, 1776, yet Benjamin Franklin received a draft for review on Friday, June 21, by which time it had already been reviewed by the drafting committee and their changes taken in on the manuscript sent to Franklin for his comments. Jefferson enclosed a note with it that makes this progression clear: "The enclosed paper has been read and with some small alterations approved of by the committee. Will Doctor Franklin be so good as to peruse it and suggest such alterations as his more enlarged view of the subject will dictate?" Jefferson also indicated that he would be returning the document to the committee the following day for their final approval.

Franklin made one momentous change to the start of the second paragraph, contributing to one of the most famous phrases of the Declaration. In Jefferson's original, it read, "We hold these truths to be sacred and undeniable." Franklin changed it to read, "We hold these truths to be self-evident." Removing the religious overtones was perfectly in keeping with the Enlightenment spirit of secularization, and made it a statement of rational fact rather than divine providence.

This rough draft of the Declaration of Independence was circulated to the members of the drafting committee. It shows Benjamin Franklin's momentous change, in the second paragraph, where he constructed the memorable phrase, "We hold these truths to be self-evident . . ." Franklin's decisive and distinctive crosshatching, which he used to score out the unwanted text, was a legacy from his days as a printer.

The Congressional Draft

Whereas the committee made few changes—"some small alterations"—Congress wielded the red pen more aggressively. It devoted three days to consideration of Jefferson's draft Declaration; the official record notes that it handled essential business at the beginning and end of the day on July 2, 3, and 4, before it turned to the "declaration on independence," as it was referred to in the record.

Although there is no account of what transpired over those three days, a comparison of Jefferson's draft as approved by the committee (see Appendix) with the final version shows that Congress deleted around one-quarter of the original.

The bulk of Congress's changes occurred in the latter half of the document. Up until the last of the grievances listed against the king, only a few words here and there were changed, mainly to tighten up the phrasing. The first substantial change occurred when Congress deleted an entire charge against the king relating to his participation in the slave trade. This was a prudent alteration, because slave ownership was widespread in the colonies, and it was inconsistent to rebuke the king for involvement in a practice on which so many colonists depended. Even at this early date in American history, slavery was a contentious and complex issue.

Congress also worked on the "British brethren" paragraph, simplifying and moderating it. Finally, the concluding paragraph was substantially rewritten, incorporating some of the text of Richard Henry Lee's July 2 speech and adding two references to God, whom Jefferson, a man of the Enlightenment, had omitted from his text.

Jefferson was deeply unhappy at the changes Congress made, referring to them as "mutilations." So frustrated was he that he made several clean copies of his own draft to show his friends, asking them to judge for themselves which was the better version: his own or that of Congress.

Thomas Jefferson resented the alterations made by Congress to his draft of the Declaration of Independence. However, few alterations were made to the first half of the Declaration, the section that is best known today.

The Declaration of Independence

Whether it is the work of one man or of a committee, the Declaration stands out as a masterpiece of prose writing, and is remembered not only because of its historical significance, but also because of its skilled use of rhetoric.

The Declaration never once mentions Parliament, which is striking because the dispute with Britain was focused on what rights Parliament had to legislate over the colonies. Rather, it focuses on relations with the monarch. This heightens the dramatic tone of the document and adds to its atmosphere of universal applicability; by staying clear of parliamentary wranglings, Jefferson clearly places the American bid for freedom in the context of a worldwide trend rejecting centralization of power in inherited monarchies. In addition, the Declaration does not assert the rights that should accrue to Americans as British citizens, which had been the cornerstone of previous presentations to Great Britain—this difference reinforces their claim for independence.

The Declaration of Independence has five parts: an introduction (the first paragraph); a preamble (the best-known section); a main body divided in two: a list of grievances and a description of the attempts at recourse (known as the British brethren section); and a conclusion.

When in the Course of human events, it becomes necessary for one people to dissolve the political bands which have connected them with another, and to assume among the powers of the earth, the separate and equal station to which the Laws of Nature and of Nature's God entitle them, a decent respect to the opinions of mankind requires that they should declare the causes which impel them to the separation.

The introduction is written in quite general terms, so that it could apply to the situation of almost any oppressed people. It puts the conflict into the context of world history, elevating what could be construed as a colonial dispute into a matter of principle acted out on the world stage. In addition it labels the Americans as "one people," clearly implying that what is at issue is not a civil war, but rather a conflict between two separate nations.

We hold these truths to be self-evident, that all men are created equal, that they are endowed by their Creator with certain unalienable Rights, that among these are Life, Liberty and the pursuit of Happiness.—That to secure these rights, Governments are instituted among

Men, deriving their just powers from the consent of the
governed,—That whenever any Form of Government
becomes destructive of these ends, it is the Right
of the People to alter or to abolish it, and to institute
new Government, laying its foundation on such
principles and organizing its powers in such form,
as to them shall seem most likely to effect their
Safety and Happiness.

The preamble—or at least the first half of it—is the most famous section of the Declaration of Independence. Jefferson offered up an astoundingly economical and elegant summary of Enlightenment principles of government. But at the same time, he also established the right of revolution, a fact little mentioned today.

He is expressing political ideals, rather than social realities. Neither women nor blacks were party to the "unalienable rights" of this manifesto. In the highly stratified colonial society, even Catholics were disenfranchised, although they could own land. But the sentiments expressed by Jefferson in the Declaration were part of the political discourse of his day, and everyone, from all strata of society, accepted them as such.

Jefferson ends the preamble by asserting that "the history of the present King of Great Britain is a history of repeated injuries and usurpations . . . To prove this, let Facts be submitted to a candid world."

These facts are presented in the list of grievances that follows. There are 28 grievances in total, presented not chronologically but thematically: 1–12 refer to abuses of executive power, such as suspending colonial laws and stationing a standing army during peacetime; 13–22 list unconstitutional measures, such as unfair taxation or trade constraints; 23–27 refer to waging of war; and the final grievance charges that the king did not respond to petitions submitted to him.

With only one exception, all the charges begin with the words "He has"; the exception begins, "He is." Although it is clear who is at fault, the charges are framed in ambiguous language, making them difficult to refute—any defender of Great Britain would first have to define the charge before refuting it, in effect admitting guilt before pleading innocence.

In addition, as the charges proceed, the language becomes more evocative. What began as an impersonal presentation of "facts" has made a gradual transition into an emotional text that invites the reader to identify with the American colonists—always referred to in the first-person plural as "we" or "us," in opposition to the king. Contrast the first of the grievances:

He has refused his Assent to Laws, the most
wholesome and necessary for the public good.

with these:

He has plundered our seas, ravaged our Coasts, burnt
our towns, and destroyed the lives of our people.
He is at this time transporting large Armies of foreign
Mercenaries to compleat the works of death, desolation

and tyranny, already begun with circumstances of
Cruelty & perfidy scarcely paralleled in the most
barbarous ages, and totally unworthy the Head of a
civilized nation.

This heightened language, almost biblical in its phrasing, was designed to draw in the reader. It was composed not only to convert any Americans still not committed to the revolution, but to sway foreign opinion in favor of the American cause.

Nor have We been wanting in attentions to our
Brittish brethren. We have warned them from time
to time of attempts by their legislature to extend an
unwarrantable jurisdiction over us. We have reminded
them of the circumstances of our emigration and
settlement here. We have appealed to their native
justice and magnanimity, and we have conjured them
by the ties of our common kindred to disavow these
usurpations, which would inevitably interrupt our
connections and correspondence. They too have been
deaf to the voice of justice and of consanguinity. We
must, therefore, acquiesce in the necessity, which
denounces our Separation, and hold them, as we hold
the rest of mankind, Enemies in War, in Peace Friends.

This paragraph, sometimes referred to as the "British brethren" section, describes the ways in which the colonists sought peacefully to rectify their situation. It uses short words and alliteration, in contrast to the rest of the document, further personalizing the address. Jefferson's original paragraph was more than twice this length, but in its economy, Congress's version gains strength and direct appeal.

Finally, with its conclusion, the Declaration comes full circle. It returns to the formal language and discourse of its beginning. In its first few words the Declaration refers to the need to "dissolve the political bands" that connect one people with another—and in the conclusion it does so emphatically, declaring "that all political connection between them [the colonies] and the State of Great Britain, is and ought to be totally dissolved." It goes on to assert those rights belonging to nations, of independent trade and alliances, before returning to a sentence that reestablishes the personal nature of the appeal: "And for the support of this Declaration, with a firm reliance on the protection of divine Providence, we mutually pledge to each other our Lives, our Fortunes and our sacred Honor."

The Dunlap Broadside

Once the text of the Declaration of Independence was agreed by Congress on July 4, the working copy of the manuscript was signed by John Hancock, president of the Continental Congress, and witnessed by Charles Thomson, secretary of the Congress. This was despite the fact that it was ratified by only 12 of the 13 colonies; the New York delegates had not yet received approval from their own assembly to vote in favor of independence.

The drafting committee's final responsibility was to arrange for the printing and distribution of the Declaration.

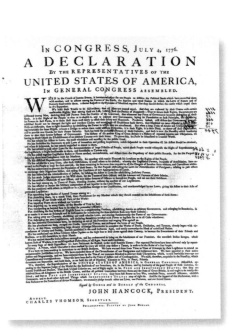

They turned to John Dunlap, one of Philadelphia's leading printers. Born in Ireland, Dunlap had arrived in Philadelphia when he was ten years old as an apprentice to his uncle, who owned a printing shop. By the time he was 21, Dunlap had set up in business on his own. In 1778 he became the official printer of the Continental Congress, printing drafts of the Constitution for use by the Convention. Later he would print the first daily newspaper in America, the *Pennsylvania Packet*.

Overnight on July 4 Dunlap printed between 200 and 500 copies of the Declaration, a version that came to be known as the Dunlap Broadside. These copies were distributed to members of the Continental Congress to be given out in their home states, as well as to the commanders of the Continental Army troops. It was also a Dunlap Broadside that was dispatched to George III.

Today only 25 copies of the Dunlap Broadside have survived. Most are held in archives and libraries, but five are in private collections. The last one to go on the block sold at auction for $8.14 million in 2000.

The Dunlap Broadside was printed on the orders of John Hancock after the text of the Declaration was approved by Congress. Unlike the signed, engrossed copy, it is not headed "The unanimous declaration ... " because the New York delegates had abstained from voting as they awaited instructions from their state assembly. The Dunlap Broadside only bears the names of John Hancock, president of the Congress, and Charles Thompson, its secretary, as befits an official Congressional proclamation.

The Signers

It was a courageous move to sign the Declaration of Independence. In effect, signing was an act of treason, and the signers were risking their lives should the bid for independence fail. After signing, it was agreed that the names of the signatories would not be made public for six months, for safety's sake. Thus an official version of the Declaration of Independence, complete with the names of the 56 signers, was not issued until January 1777. This version, known as the Goddard Broadside, was printed in Philadelphia by Mary Katharine Goddard, and only nine copies are still in existence. The Goddard Broadside marked the first time that the names of the signers were made public.

Contrary to popular belief today, the Declaration was not signed on July 4, 1776. One reason for the delay in signing was that the Declaration did not become unanimous until July 19, when New York finally authorized its delegates to approve independence. The vote was unanimous by state delegation, not individuals, with some members of Congress either abstaining or even voting against the Declaration. Later some of these men, such as George Read of Delaware (who voted against it) and Robert Morris of Pennsylvania (who abstained), still signed.

It was only once the vote was unanimous that Congress ordered an engrossed copy to be prepared for signature, headed with the words "The unanimous declaration of the thirteen United States of America." An "engrossed copy" refers to the official document, handwritten on parchment. This was probably scripted by

The Declaration of Independence was signed in the Assembly Room of the State House in Philadelphia, today known as Independence Hall. Most of the signers were able to gather in person on August 23, 1776, and space was left for those who were unable to attend.

Thomas Matlack from Pennsylvania, an assistant to Charles Thomson, who had earlier written out George Washington's commission as general of the Continental Army. Recognizing the historical significance of the document, they consulted with Torah scribes in America to ascertain which type of ink would be the longest lasting. It took Matlack until August 2 to finish the process.

As president of the Continental Congress, John Hancock was the first to sign the Declaration of Independence, and his elegant and distinctive signature is immediately recognizable today.

Most of the signers gathered on August 2 in the Assembly Room of the State House in Philadelphia. John Hancock, as president of the Congress, was the first person to sign, his bold signature centered below the text. It is said that Hancock signed so large as a show of defiance— George III had quite poor vision, and Hancock joked that his name was now big enough to be seen by the king even without his reading glasses. As Hancock signed, he said, "There must be no pulling different ways. We must all hang together." And Benjamin Franklin quipped, "Yes, we must, indeed, hang together, or most assuredly we shall all hang separately."

The other members of Congress then followed, in order of states, with New Hampshire (the northernmost state) topping the list on the right-hand side, and Georgia (the one farthest south) at the end and on the left. Space was left for the members of Congress who were not able to attend the meeting (although Matthew Thornton of New Hampshire did not have enough room to fit his name and had to sign elsewhere). Delegates had a variety of reasons for missing the August 2 ceremony: for example, Oliver

the Declaration of Independence
on this relief panel, one of four
from the pedestal of a statue
of Franklin found by Boston's
Old City Hall.

Wolcott of Connecticut and Thomas McKean of Delaware were with the army.

Some delegates of the Continental Congress never put their name to the document. For instance, Robert R. Livingston of New York, despite being on the drafting committee, did not sign, believing that the Declaration was being issued too soon. John Dickinson of Pennsylvania— respected as one of the authors of the Declaration of the Causes and Necessity of Taking Up Arms—nonetheless held out hope of reconciliation; it had been on his instigation that the futile Olive Branch Petition had been sent to George III. Despite his profound reservations, Dickinson enlisted with George Washington as a private, rising through the ranks to become brigadier-general of the Pennsylvania militia.

The signers were a high-profile group with a deep commitment to public service. At the time of signing they were on the whole quite young, with an average age of just 45, and so they had many years ahead of them. Benjamin Franklin was the eldest, aged 70; the youngest, Thomas Lynch, was only 27.

Many participated in politics on the national level. Thomas Jefferson, John Adams, and Elbridge Gerry each became vice president, and John Adams and Thomas Jefferson became president. Six signers—Roger Sherman, Robert Morris, Benjamin Franklin, George Clymer, James Wilson, and George Reed—also signed the United States Constitution (Elbridge Gerry attended the federal convention,

Charles Carroll of Carrollton, in Maryland, one of the signers of the Declaration of Independence, was reputed to be the richest man in the American colonies.

but refused to sign the Constitution). Seven entered the House of Representatives, and six were senators. James Wilson and Samuel Chase became Justices of the United States Supreme Court. On the state level, 15 signers participated in their state constitutional conventions, 13 became governors, 18 served in state legislatures, and 16 became state and federal judges.

They were all members of the American elite, professionals and landowners—Charles Carroll of Maryland was reputed to be the richest man in America—and many were well educated. Seven studied at Harvard, four each at Yale and William & Mary, and three at Princeton. George Wythe, a professor at William & Mary, had been one of Thomas Jefferson's law instructors. Five signers helped to establish institutes of higher learning: Benjamin Franklin at the University of Pennsylvania; Thomas Jefferson at the University of Virginia; Benjamin Rush at Dickinson College; Lewis Morris at New York University; and George Walton at the University of Georgia.

Seventeen of the signers risked their lives not just as signers, but also by joining the Continental Army. Five were captured by the British during the war, and nine of the signers died in the war. Others, and their families, were targeted by British forces. Thomas McKean of Delaware wrote that he was "hunted like a fox" throughout the war. Twelve signers lost their homes and property to looting during the war.

IN CONGRESS, July 4, 1776.

The unanimous Declaration of the thirteen united States of America,

When in the Course of human events, it becomes necessary for one people to dissolve the political bands which have connected them with another, and to assume among the powers of the earth, the separate and equal station to which the Laws of Nature and of Nature's God entitle them, a decent respect to the opinions of mankind requires that they should declare the causes which impel them to the separation.

We hold these truths to be self-evident, that all men are created equal, that they are endowed by their Creator with certain unalienable Rights, that among these are Life, Liberty and the pursuit of Happiness.—That to secure these rights, Governments are instituted among Men, deriving their just powers from the consent of the governed,—That whenever any Form of Government becomes destructive of these ends, it is the Right of the People to alter or to abolish it, and to institute new Government, laying its foundation on such principles and organizing its powers in such form, as to them shall seem most likely to effect their Safety and Happiness. Prudence, indeed, will dictate that Governments long established should not be changed for light and transient causes; and accordingly all experience hath shewn, that mankind are more disposed to suffer, while evils are sufferable, than to right themselves by abolishing the forms to which they are accustomed. But when a long train of abuses and usurpations, pursuing invariably the same Object evinces a design to reduce them under absolute Despotism, it is their right, it is their duty, to throw off such Government, and to provide new Guards for their future security.—Such has been the patient sufferance of these Colonies; and such is now the necessity which constrains them to alter their former Systems of Government. The history of the present King of Great Britain is a history of repeated injuries and usurpations, all having in direct object the establishment of an absolute Tyranny over these States. To prove this, let Facts be submitted to a candid world.

the Supreme Judge of the world for the rectitude of our in.

are, and of Right ought to be Free and Independent

Great Britain; is and ought to be totally dissolved; and

to all other Acts and Things which Independent

we mutually pledge to each other our Lives, our Fortunes

He has refused his Assent to Laws, the most wholesome and necessary for the public good.

He has forbidden his Governors to pass Laws of immediate and pressing importance, unless suspended in their operation till his Assent should be obtained; and when so suspended, he has utterly neglected to attend to them.

He has refused to pass other Laws for the accommodation of large districts of people, unless those people would relinquish the right of Representation in the Legislature, a right inestimable to them and formidable to tyrants only.

He has called together legislative bodies at places unusual, uncomfortable, and distant from the depository of their public Records, for the sole purpose of fatiguing them into compliance with his measures.

He has dissolved Representative Houses repeatedly, for opposing with manly firmness his invasions on the rights of the people.

He has refused for a long time, after such dissolutions, to cause others to be elected; whereby the Legislative powers, incapable of Annihilation, have returned to the People at large for their exercise; the State remaining in the mean time exposed to all the dangers of invasion from without, and convulsions within.

He has endeavoured to prevent the population of these States; for that purpose obstructing the Laws for Naturalization of Foreigners; refusing to pass others to encourage their migrations hither, and raising the conditions of new Appropriations of Lands.

He has obstructed the Administration of Justice, by refusing his Assent to Laws for establishing Judiciary powers.

He has made Judges dependent on his Will alone, for the tenure of their offices, and the amount and payment of their salaries.

He has erected a multitude of New Offices, and sent hither swarms of Officers to harrass our people, and eat out their substance.

He has kept among us, in times of peace, Standing Armies without the Consent of our legislatures.

He has affected to render the Military independent of and superior to the Civil power.

He has combined with others to subject us to a jurisdiction foreign to our constitution, and unacknowledged by our laws; giving his Assent to their Acts of pretended Legislation:

For Quartering large bodies of armed troops among us:

For protecting them, by a mock Trial, from punishment for any Murders which they should commit on the Inhabitants of these States:

For cutting off our Trade with all parts of the world:

For imposing Taxes on us without our Consent:

For depriving us in many cases, of the benefits of Trial by Jury:

For transporting us beyond Seas to be tried for pretended offences:

For abolishing the free System of English Laws in a neighbouring Province, establishing therein an Arbitrary government, and enlarging its Boundaries so as to render it at once an example and fit instrument for introducing the same absolute rule into these Colonies:

For taking away our Charters, abolishing our most valuable Laws, and altering fundamentally the Forms of our Governments:

For suspending our own Legislatures, and declaring themselves invested with power to legislate for us in all cases whatsoever.

the Supreme Judge of the world for the rectitude of our in.
are, and of Right ought tobe *Free and Independent*
reat Britain, is and ought to be totally dissolved; and
do all other Acts and Things which Independent
we mutually pledge to each other our Lives, our Fortunes

He has abdicated Government here, by declaring us out of his Protection and waging War against us.

He has plundered our seas, ravaged our Coasts, burnt our towns, and destroyed the lives of our people.

He is at this time transporting large Armies of foreign Mercenaries to compleat the works of death, desolation and tyranny, already begun with circumstances of Cruelty & perfidy scarcely paralleled in the most barbarous ages, and totally unworthy the Head of a civilized nation.

He has constrained our fellow Citizens taken Captive on the high Seas to bear Arms against their Country, to become the executioners of their friends and Brethren, or to fall themselves by their Hands.

He has excited domestic insurrections amongst us, and has endeavoured to bring on the inhabitants of our frontiers, the merciless Indian Savages, whose known rule of warfare, is an undistinguished destruction of all ages, sexes and conditions.

In every stage of these Oppressions We have Petitioned for Redress in the most humble terms: Our repeated Petitions have been answered only by repeated injury. A Prince whose character is thus marked by every act which may define a Tyrant, is unfit to be the ruler of a free people.

Nor have We been wanting in attentions to our Brittish brethren. We have warned them from time to time of attempts by their legislature to extend an unwarrantable jurisdiction over us. We have reminded them of the circumstances of our emigration and settlement here. We have appealed to their native justice and magnanimity, and we have conjured them by the ties of our common kindred to disavow these usurpations, which, would inevitably interrupt our connections and correspondence. They too have been deaf to the voice of justice and of consanguinity. We must, therefore, acquiesce in the necessity, which denounces our Separation, and hold them, as we hold the rest of mankind, Enemies in War, in Peace Friends.

We, therefore, the Representatives of the united States of America, in General Congress, Assembled, appealing to the Supreme Judge of the world for the rectitude of our intentions, do, in the Name, and by Authority of the good People of these Colonies, solemnly publish and declare, That these United Colonies are, and of Right ought to be Free and Independent States; that they are Absolved from all Allegiance to the British Crown, and that all political connection between them and the State of Great Britain, is and ought to be totally dissolved; and that as Free and Independent States, they have full Power to levy War, conclude Peace, contract Alliances, establish Commerce, and to do all other Acts and Things which Independent States may of right do. And for the support of this Declaration, with a firm reliance on the protection of divine Providence, we mutually pledge to each other our Lives, our Fortunes and our sacred Honor.

This decorative lithograph, reproducing portraits of the framers and signers of the Declaration of Independence, along with their signatures, was made in 1874, at a time when the Declaration of Independence was again venerated in the U.S.

The 56 signatures on the Declaration of Independence appear in these positions:

Column 1
Georgia:
Button Gwinnett
Lyman Hall
George Walton

Column 2
North Carolina:
William Hooper
Joseph Hewes
John Penn
South Carolina:
Edward Rutledge
Thomas Heyward, Jr.
Thomas Lynch, Jr.
Arthur Middleton

Column 3
Massachusetts:
John Hancock
Maryland:
Samuel Chase
William Paca
Thomas Stone
Charles Carroll of Carrollton
Virginia:
George Wythe
Richard Henry Lee
Thomas Jefferson

Benjamin Harrison
Thomas Nelson, Jr.
Francis Lightfoot Lee
Carter Braxton

Column 4
Pennsylvania:
Robert Morris
Benjamin Rush
Benjamin Franklin
John Morton
George Clymer
James Smith
George Taylor
James Wilson
George Ross
Delaware:
Caesar Rodney
George Read
Thomas McKean

Column 5
New York:
William Floyd
Philip Livingston
Francis Lewis
Lewis Morris
New Jersey:
Richard Stockton

John Witherspoon
Francis Hopkinson
John Hart
Abraham Clark

Column 6
New Hampshire:
Josiah Bartlett
William Whipple
Massachusetts:
Samuel Adams
John Adams
Robert Treat Paine
Elbridge Gerry
Rhode Island:
Stephen Hopkins
William Ellery
Connecticut:
Roger Sherman
Samuel Huntington
William Williams
Oliver Wolcott
New Hampshire:
Matthew Thornton

UNDERSTANDING THE
DECLARATION OF INDEPENDENCE
IMMEDIATE
IMPACT

I am well aware of the Toil and Blood and Treasure, that it will cost Us to maintain this Declaration, and support and defend these States. Yet through all the Gloom I can see the Rays of ravishing Light and Glory. I can see that the End is more than worth all the Means. And that Posterity will tryumph in that Days Transaction.

John Adams to his wife, Abigail, July 2, 1776

As soon as the copies of the Dunlap Broadside rolled off the presses, they were dispatched throughout the colonies, directed to prominent politicians, and community and religious leaders. John Hancock, as president of the Continental Congress, attached a letter to each recipient, "to request that you will have it proclaimed in your Colony in the way you shall think most proper." In addition, copies were sent to George Washington, so that it could be read to those men serving in the Continental Army.

The aim was not only to spread the news, but also to inspire and motivate Americans throughout the colonies to support the war effort. In particular, Washington and others hoped that the announcement of the Declaration of Independence would encourage more men to enlist in the army. Now that relations between the two countries had been clearly defined as two nations at war, enlistment was no longer an act of treason against the British government. Whereas the British had a professional army and could call upon as many as 50,000 troops as well as hire German mercenaries, the American had as few as 5,000 men with

Following a request from John Hancock, George Washington had the text of the Declaration of Independence read out to his troops in New York, within earshot of the British army.

little or no experience of war, supported by small state militias.

Public Celebration

Word of independence—and of the Declaration of Independence—spread quickly. The first newspaper to publish it

The first American centennial celebration in 1876 was commemorated by readings of the Declaration of Independence throughout the country. This commemoration took place in Minnesota.

was the *Pennsylvania Evening Post* on July 6, and other journals and newspapers soon followed: by the end of July it had been printed in full in more than 30 newspapers. It was even translated into German to be printed in Pennsylvania's German-language paper (this translation was also the first to appear in the German press in Europe). Some papers ran it as part of the main text, and others devoted a full page to it, creating a poster that could be publicly displayed.

State officials were agreed that the best way to spread the news was by means of public readings of the Declaration. The first readings took place on July 8 in Philadelphia and Easton, Pennsylvania, and in Trenton, New Jersey. On July 9 George Washington ordered readings to take place to the troops in New York City, within easy earshot of the British army. Public readings continued to be held into August, as the text of the Declaration of Independence traveled throughout the colonies and out into the countryside. And the text made for good reading: Jefferson seems to have had public readings in mind as he composed it, and one of his drafts is marked up with notations, as if for an orator.

John Adams maintained throughout his life that commemorative celebrations should take place on July 2 (the day on which independence was declared) rather than on July 4 (the day on which the text of the Declaration was ratified).

Public readings were invariably accompanied by great festivities, including parades, concerts, the firing of cannons and muskets, and even fireworks. As the *Virginia Gazette* reported, "The declaration, and other proceedings, were received with loud acclamations." Enthusiastic crowds destroyed images associated with Britain, such as pictures of King George III or British flags. In New York City a grand equestrian statue of George III was pulled down by a mob and its lead later melted to make bullets.

That independence was a matter for celebration was in no doubt. On July 2, 1776, John Adams had written to his wife, Abigail, suggesting that the day on which Congress declared independence would be celebrated in perpetuity:

> *I am apt to believe that it will be celebrated, by succeeding Generations, as the great anniversary Festival. It ought to be commemorated, as the Day of Deliverance by solemn Acts of Devotion to God Almighty. It ought to be solemnized with Pomp and Parade, with Shews, Games, Sports, Guns, Bells, Bonfires, and Illuminations from one End of this Continent to the other from this Time forward forever more.*

But Adams believed that the memorable date was July 2, the day on which Congress passed the vote, rather than July 4, the date on which the text of the Declaration of Independence was approved. Well into his old age he maintained this view, often turning down invitations to appear at July 4 events because he believed the celebrations were taking place on the wrong day.

By the mid-nineteenth century, July 4 celebrations had become quite lavish, as is seen here, when local government officials celebrated Independence Day at Faneuil Hall in Boston, Massachusetts, in 1853.

The following year Philadelphia held the first-ever organized celebration of American independence, on July 4, the date of Congress's approval of the Declaration. Congress, much occupied with the war, had neglected to make any plans to commemorate the anniversary. In fact, it was not until July 2 itself that members of Congress pointed out the significance of the day, by which time it was too late to organize anything.

So it was by chance that the first celebrations of American independence took place on July 4. By the following year, however, the July 4 celebration was already well established. On that day in 1778 George Washington issued double rations of rum to all his soldiers to mark the occasion, and John Adams and Benjamin Franklin held a dinner in Paris for expatriate Americans. In 1781 Massachusetts became the first state to make the date an official state holiday; it did not become an official federal holiday until 1941.

Over the years, as Independence Day came to be celebrated throughout the country, the fact that July 4 commemorated the Declaration of Independence, rather than independence itself, was forgotten. Public readings played no part in early anniversary celebrations, which were dominated instead by parades, speeches, and toasts. The tradition of reading out the Declaration of Independence on July 4 did not begin until after the War of 1812, when annual celebrations, with fireworks and grand pagentry, became commonplace.

General John Burgoyne's British troops, poorly equipped and small in number, could not withstand rigorous American resistance, and he surrendered in Saratoga, New York, in October 1777. This represented a serious setback for the British.

Safeguarding the Declaration

As Congress traveled to safe havens throughout the war, the engrossed copy of the Declaration of Independence traveled along too. When the early course of the war did not go well for the American army, Congress was forced to relocate from Philadelphia to Baltimore in December 1776. Although Congress returned to Philadelphia in March 1777, it could not remain there for long, as the British began their advance on the city in the summer, finally occupying it on September 26. Congress moved out again—to Lancaster, Pennsylvania, for a day on September 25, and eventually to York, Pennsylvania, where it remained from September 27, 1777, to June 1778.

Meanwhile, in October 1777 the British army experienced a major defeat in the north, with General Burgoyne surrendering his entire army at Saratoga. Apprehensive about the course the war was taking, the British government framed an offer to the Americans: a return to the status quo of 1763, meaning autonomous colonial status, with no taxation levied by Britain; the repeal of any acts detrimental to American commerce; and no standing army.

Benjamin Franklin, the American ambassador in Paris, had no intention of accepting the British offer, since he was totally committed to achieving full independence. However, he had no compunction about using it as leverage to bring the French on board on the American side. Concerned that a new alliance with America would revitalize the British, their old rivals, the French government finally offered aid and assistance on an official footing. On February 6, 1778, Franklin signed two treaties with the government of Louis XVI: a commercial treaty, and a military alliance (in fact, this proved to be the only military alliance America was to sign until the NATO pact in 1949). In this way, the Declaration of Independence achieved one of its stated aims: "to . . . contract alliances, establish commerce & to do all other acts & things which independent states may of right do."

Congress was forced to flee from its headquarters in the State House in Philadelphia, seen here, when the fighting became too close for comfort. The Declaration of Independence traveled with the government from one safe haven to another.

These treaties radically changed the course of the war. With France on its side, America was also now supported by its ally, Spain, and soon enough the Netherlands and Russia were embroiled in the distant conflict too. The theater of war now extended as far east as India, north into Canada, and south into the Caribbean, and Britain was isolated diplomatically and overstretched militarily.

By the spring of 1778 British forces had left Philadelphia in an attempt to regroup in New York, and Congress was able to return to the city, with the Declaration of Independence. There it remained safely throughout the rest of the war. The last battle in the Revolutionary War on American soil took place on November 10, 1782.

The Treaty of Paris

With the Treaty of Paris in September 1783, which officially ended the war with Britain, the Declaration of Independence achieved its key aim—that of independence from Britain. Although Congress had voted for independence on July 2,

1776, and with the Declaration announced that decision to the world, that did not actually mean that the American colonies were independent. As British philosopher Jeremy Bentham wrote in his hostile "Short Review of the Declaration" in 1776, "[I]t is one thing for them to say, the connection, which bound them to us, is dissolved, another to dissolve it; . . . to accomplish their independence is not quite so easy as to declare it." It was not until the treaty was signed with Britain that independence was officially granted and thus recognized in international law.

Benjamin Franklin, John Adams, and John Jay of New York (a delegate to both Continental Congresses, though he did not sign the Declaration of Independence) were the principal negotiators for the American side, and the discussions were long and arduous, especially as Britain was signing treaties simultaneously with France and Spain. Although America had promised France that it would not negotiate independently, and would submit offers for approval, Franklin, Adams, and Jay boldly decided to negotiate separately, despite the alliance. Only the issue of American independence was not contentious—all parties accepted that as a given.

Article 1:

His Brittanic Majesty acknowledges the said United States, viz., New Hampshire, Massachusetts Bay, Rhode Island and Providence Plantations, Connecticut, New York, New Jersey, Pennsylvania, Maryland, Virginia, North Carolina, South Carolina and Georgia, to be free

*sovereign and independent states, that he treats with
them as such, and for himself, his heirs, and successors,
relinquishes all claims to the government, propriety, and
territorial rights of the same and every part thereof.*

The Treaty of Paris also established the borders of
America and defined British, French, and Spanish territory in
North America. Although the new American republic won
lands extending as far west as the Mississippi River, most of
the west and the south went to Spain, with Britain retaining
Canada, and France preserving its Caribbean colonies. The
treaty also had clauses, which would prove impossible to
enforce, relating to war debts and restitution: it guaranteed
no impediment to reclaiming war debts; offered restitution to
British subjects of goods confiscated during the war;
recommended that Congress request that the states annul
any laws legalizing such confiscation; and sought to protect
the rights and safety of American loyalists.

Establishing Government

Throughout the war the business of government had to
continue. Starting from May 1776, after Congress instructed
them to do so, individual states began drawing up their own
constitutions, to fill the vacuum left by the withdrawal of
British authority. It was no easy process. Although most
states managed to complete the task within a year of the
Declaration of Independence, it took Massachusetts until
1780, and Connecticut and Rhode Island issued constitutions
that scarcely differed from their original colonial charters.

John Dickinson wrote the draft text that became the basis of the Articles of Confederation. Long active in American politics, he was one of the most prominent conservatives.

Individual rights were paramount to the framers of the state constitutions. Each document began with some kind of Bill of Rights, guaranteeing fundamental individual rights. The Virginia Declaration of Rights, which inspired Jefferson as he wrote the Declaration of Independence, was a model for those of many other states. Suffrage was also broadened, with representation usually based on population, but with few exceptions property ownership was still considered a prerequisite not only for voting, but also for holding public office.

The state constitutions were careful to avoid the centralization of power inherent in the British system of colonial government. The powers of the elected governor, as the chief executive of the state, were limited, whereas those of the elected assemblies were strengthened. In addition assemblies generally appointed the cabinet, the advisory body that worked with the governor, for further accountability. The constitution of Pennsylvania, the most radical of the 13 new constitutions, abolished the position of governor altogether, devolving authority to a council elected by the state assembly (itself elected). The system of checks and balances among the three branches of government—the executive, legislative, and judicial—was fundamental to all the new constitutions.

The Articles of Confederation

Although the Continental Congress had been acting as a federal government from the time of its formation, it had no real authority to do so, and it needed to create a legal basis for its existence and activity. A committee to draft Articles of Confederation was appointed on the same day as the drafting committee for the Declaration of Independence. After long debate, the Articles of Confederation, drafted by John Dickinson but much amended by Congress, were approved in November 1777 and submitted to the states for their ratification. And although the states retained much autonomy, including all rights to levy taxes and to manage their own commerce and trade, the Articles were not unanimously ratified until 1781, by which time their limitations were already showing.

The states were far more autonomous than they are today—in effect, they were virtually separate countries, each with its own founding document, culture, and infrastructure. Seen in this context, the fact they could unite philosophically, emotionally, and practically to wage war against Britain was quite an achievement. But formally defining the union, without imposing on individual states' rights, was extremely delicate, because the idea of a formal union with centralized powers was anathema to the American colonies, struggling to free themselves from the oppression they believed arose from just such centralization of power.

The Articles of Confederation, therefore, were conservative and cautious. In effect, they simply transferred to Congress the powers that had once belonged to the king in terms of international relations and Native American affairs, as well as the management of weights and measures and the post office, and the issuance of money. It was up to the states to decide how many delegates to send to Congress, but irrespective of the number of delegates, each state had only one vote, and a majority of nine was required to pass any act. Members of Congress were not paid and were forbidden to take any remunerated public office; in effect, becoming a Congressional representative became the province of the independently wealthy élite.

Crucially—and understandably, considering that the issue of taxation was a central cause of the war now under way—Congress was not empowered to levy taxes on a national basis. So although it was empowered to wage war and run a rudimentary national infrastructure, it was not provided with an official means of funding its activities. Instead it had to depend on requisition money given by the states, which in practice were rarely paid.

The Constitution

By the time of the Treaty of Paris, the United States of America may have been independent, but the states were hardly united. The Articles of Confederation had created such a loose union that it was close to fracturing. Congress had a clear role to play in coordinating the war effort, but once the war ended, interest waned as the states began to act autonomously. Political leaders focused their attention on governing their home states, and Congress became aimless.

The situation for the fledgling nation was dire. Congress had no means of raising money to fund its own operations or to service or pay off its foreign debt. Because it had no control over commerce, it could not negotiate further foreign trade, and the states began feuding among themselves for whatever international business trickled their way. The economic depression that followed the end of the war heightened tensions. Congress could not even ensure that the states respected the terms of the Treaty of Paris, regarding restitution for confiscated loyalist estates and unpaid business debts. Because of this, America's standing in the international arena suffered. No foreign nation wanted to enter into agreements with a government that could not enforce existing international treaties or pay off its existing debts.

The same discord was taking place on the level of the state governments. The early state constitutions, reacting against their historical circumstance, had granted far too much power to popular legislatures, which had become bloated, expensive, and inefficient. So in the 1780s many states began the process of revising their constitutions to restore some balance, strengthening the executive and judicial branches of government.

Throughout the country a new generation of nationalists was rising through the political ranks. However, their nationalism took a different form from the previous generation's. Whereas in the 1760s and 1770s nationalism was all about winning independence and instituting government based on popular democracy, the 1780s focus was on establishing security by strengthening central government.

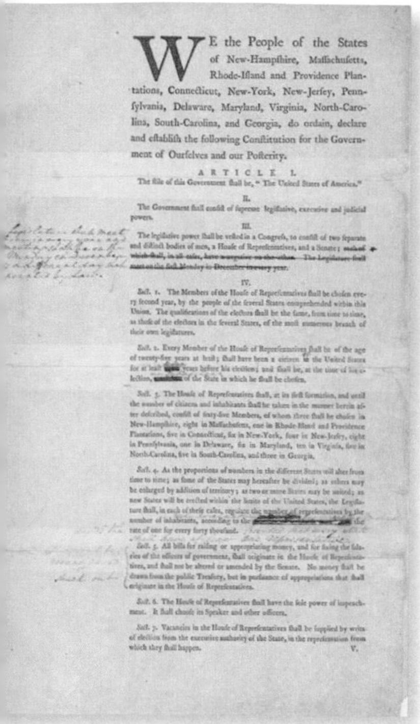

WE the People of the States of New-Hampshire, Massachusetts, Rhode-Island and Providence Plantations, Connecticut, New-York, New-Jersey, Pennsylvania, Delaware, Maryland, Virginia, North-Carolina, South-Carolina, and Georgia, do ordain, declare and establish the following Constitution for the Government of Ourselves and our Posterity.

ARTICLE I.

The stile of this Government shall be, "The United States of America."

II.

The Government shall consist of supreme legislative, executive and judicial powers.

III.

The legislative power shall be vested in a Congress, to consist of two separate and distinct bodies of men, a House of Representatives, and a Senate; each of which shall, in all cases, have a negative on the other. The Legislature shall meet on the first Monday in December in every year.

IV.

Sect. 1. The Members of the House of Representatives shall be chosen every second year, by the people of the several States comprehended within this Union. The qualifications of the electors shall be the same, from time to time, as those of the electors in the several States, of the most numerous branch of their own legislatures.

Sect. 2. Every Member of the House of Representatives shall be of the age of twenty-five years at least; shall have been a citizen in the United States for at least [illegible] years before his election; and shall be, at the time of his election, [illegible] of the State in which he shall be chosen.

Sect. 3. The House of Representatives shall, at its first formation, and until the number of citizens and inhabitants shall be taken in the manner herein after described, consist of sixty-five Members, of whom three shall be chosen in New-Hampshire, eight in Massachusetts, one in Rhode-Island and Providence Plantations, five in Connecticut, six in New-York, four in New-Jersey, eight in Pennsylvania, one in Delaware, six in Maryland, ten in Virginia, five in North-Carolina, five in South-Carolina, and three in Georgia.

Sect. 4. As the proportions of numbers in the different States will alter from time to time; as some of the States may hereafter be divided; as others may be enlarged by addition of territory; as two or more States may be united; as new States will be erected within the limits of the United States, the Legislature shall, in each of these cases, regulate the number of representatives by the number of inhabitants, according to the [illegible] the rate of one for every forty thousand.

Sect. 5. All bills for raising or appropriating money, and for fixing the salaries of the officers of government, shall originate in the House of Representatives, and shall not be altered or amended by the Senate. No money shall be drawn from the public Treasury, but in pursuance of appropriations that shall originate in the House of Representatives.

Sect. 6. The House of Representatives shall have the sole power of impeachment. It shall choose its Speaker and other officers.

Sect. 7. Vacancies in the House of Representatives shall be supplied by writs of election from the executive authority of the State, in the representation from which they shall happen.

V.

Top: Patrick Henry, one of the most active patriots during the fight for independence, declined to attend the Confederation Congress that produced the U.S. Constitution.

Above: the Constitution is the foundation stone of the American government and U.S. law.

These pressures led to the call for a Confederation Congress, authorized by Congress to revise the Articles of Confederation. It convened in Philadelphia on May 25, 1787, meeting in the same room in which the Declaration of Independence was signed. Fifty-five delegates from 12 states attended—only Rhode Island abstained. The delegates were well educated and experienced. Among them they had experience of serving in Congress, in their state constitutional conventions, and even as state governor. They were also young—their average age was just 42. The oldest delegates included some venerable names: George Mason, Roger Sherman, and Benjamin Franklin (at the age of 81 the oldest delegate). Many of the revolutionary leaders of the 1770s were conspicuously absent: Jefferson and John Adams were in Europe; Samuel Adams was unwell; Richard Henry Lee and Patrick Henry declined to attend.

From May to September the delegates debated profoundly, fearlessly, and furiously. The conclusion they unveiled on September 17—the new Constitution—was as radical a statement as the Declaration of Independence was in its time. Its departure from the status quo of the Articles of Confederation was an attempt by the framers to force the new American nation to live up to its potential, as envisaged by the revolutionaries of the 1770s. It created a new structure for the federal government, with limited but sufficient powers and the ability to enforce its law. Rather than the states ruling supreme within a loose umbrella structure, they retained many rights within a strengthened union.

We the People of the United States, in Order to form a more perfect Union, establish Justice, insure domestic Tranquility, provide for the common defence, promote the general Welfare, and secure the Blessings of Liberty to ourselves and our Posterity, do ordain and establish this Constitution for the United States of America.

The Constitution is the founding and fundamental document of American government, and thus of the United States of America. All law derives from the Constitution, either directly or through interpretation and elucidation of the text. It is studied, analyzed, and wrangled over by lawyers and constitutional scholars. Yet despite its great significance, both historical and contemporary, it receives none of the popular attention that the Declaration does. Its anniversary, September 17, is not commemorated with public celebrations; although the president does a public reading annually, it is not televised and takes place with little pomp or ceremony.

One reason why the Constitution has not captured the popular imagination is that it does not benefit from Jefferson's artfully constructed prose or his ability to summarize essential truths. However, the Declaration of Independence was really just a glorious announcement. It contained no means to put into effect the practical measures that it mentions in its final paragraph, or even to achieve its aims. It therefore had the luxury of eloquence. The Constitution, on the other hand, was—and is—a working document. Although it represented a revolutionary break with the past, just as the Declaration did, it also laid the practical groundwork for the future.

UNDERSTANDING THE DECLARATION OF INDEPENDENCE
THE DECLARATION'S LEGACY

The publication of this document as well as the proclamation of a formal war against Great Britain offer evidence of the courage of the leadership there.

Vasili Grigorevich Lizakevich, Russian chargé d'affaires

in London, August 13, 1776

The Continental Congress's submission to a candid world was met by an ominous silence from its foreign audience. Although its framers had great ambitions, the Declaration of Independence itself achieved little in the short term. Rather, the progress of the war, along with concerted diplomacy, ultimately achieved the stated goal of independence. In the longer term, the Declaration made its influence felt on the international scene, and then in some very surprising places.

The British Reception

The text of the Declaration of Independence made it across the Atlantic in short order. Four copies were recorded in British state papers by the fall of 1776. From mid-August the text also started to appear in British newspapers, reprinted in full, though usually on the back page and without much by way of introduction or commentary. Its publication inspired little debate; there were few editorials, or even letters to the editor on the subject, in the normally vociferous British press.

Nor did the British government offer any direct response to the Declaration of Independence, in part because to refute it or deny it would be to acknowledge its legitimacy. Thus no mention was made in Parliament of the Declaration of Independence. However, the government did commission a rebuttal of the Declaration from a young lawyer named John Lind, who had earlier written two pamphlets about government and the American colonies. Over some 100 pages in the "Answer to the Declaration of the American Congress" of 1776, Lind offered a point-by-point refutation of the Declaration, mocking its aims, its argument, and the American people themselves. Although he focused largely on the section detailing the accusations against the king, he also turned his attention to the preamble, albeit reluctantly:

> Of the preamble I have taken little notice. The truth is, little or none deserve. The opinions of modern Americans on Government, like those of good ancestors on witchcraft, would be too ridiculous . . . , contemptible and extravagant as they be, had they not led to most serious evils.
>
> In this preamble however It is, that they attempt to establish a theory of Government; a theory, as absurd and visionary, as the system of conduct in defence of which It is established, is nefarious. Here it is, that maxims are advanced in justification of their enterprises against the British Government. To these maxims, adduced for this purpose, it would be sufficient to say, that they are repugnant to the British Constitution. But beyond this they are subversive to every actual or Imaginable kind of Government.

Lind's work was accompanied by a 50-page essay, "A Short Review of the Declaration," which set out to destroy

The British philosopher Jeremy Bentham was one of the few opponents of the Declaration of Independence in Britain to put his ideas down on paper, although his diatribe against the document, "A Short Review of the Declaration," was published anonymously.

the logical underpinnings of the Declaration. It was written, anonymously, by Jeremy Bentham, the British philosopher and founder of utilitarianism. A friend of Lind's, Bentham had earlier assisted him on his other pamphlets about the colonies. Bentham was a determined opponent of the idea of natural rights or natural law, which he referred to throughout his life as "simple nonsense." To Bentham, the only laws were those created by legislators in an official capacity, and the only rights possessed by man were those granted by such laws. As he asserted anonymously, "If to what they now demand they were entitled by any law of God, they had only to produce that law, and all controversy was at an end. Instead of this, what do they produce? What they call self-evident truths." Although he was no foe of America, or even necessarily an opponent of its desire to achieve independence, Bentham believed the preamble was a fatal weakness, not only of the Declaration but of the complete undertaking. As he wrote in 1780, "Who can help lamenting, that so rational a cause should be rested upon reasons, so much fitter to beget objections, than to remove them?"

The only other official response to the Declaration of Independence came from the pen of Thomas Hutchinson, an American loyalist residing in England. He had been lieutenant governor of the colony of Massachusetts during the Boston Massacre and governor during the Boston Tea Party. Branded a traitor for his support of the monarchy, he was twice attacked by mobs and his home looted, and for the safety of his family and himself he moved to England after 1773. In

Boston, seen here in a view from 1764, was home to Thomas Hutchinson, who was forced to move to England in 1774 after he and his family were attacked because of his loyalist views.

"Strictures upon the Declaration of the Congress at Philadelphia" (1776), he too criticized the list of grievances. "I thought there would have been more policy in leaving the World altogether ignorant of the motives to this Rebellion, than in offering such false and frivolous reasons in support of it," he claimed, complaining that the ambiguous way in which the charges were framed was designed simply to cover up their weakness. In his view, the charges in reality carried little weight and were presented only to give some basis for the actions of a small group of rebels:

> [T]here were men in each of the principal Colonies, who had Independence in view, before any of those Taxes were laid, or proposed, which have since been the ostensible cause of resisting the execution of the Acts of Parliament. Those men have conducted the Rebellion in the several stages of it, until they have removed the constitutional powers of Government in each Colony, and have assumed to themselves, with others, a supreme authority over the whole.

What the Declaration of Independence failed to achieve, the progress of the war made real. As the tide turned militarily against the British forces, culminating in Burgoyne's surrender after the battle of Saratoga, the British government and the British people both began to conceive of the Americans not as unruly children who needed to be disciplined, but rather as a belligerent nation at war. The alliance with France that followed in March 1778 completed this process. The Americans had much in common with the British, including a shared religion and culture and a political commitment to limited central government, and this created a special bond between the two. The French, on the other hand, were not only rivals on the international stage, but culturally very different, both in terms of their language and culture and in their system of government. From this point on, the British government began to negotiate with the Americans as a separate and independent nation; the change in public attitude was evidenced by a different treatment in the newspapers, as America became just another theater of war in the newly expanded conflict.

France

France was as silent as Britain immediately after the Declaration of Independence was published in 1776. The first copy sent to Silas Deane, the American representative in Paris, was lost at sea, and the second did not arrive until November of that year. Again it received no response, and again American military success was more influential in changing opinion and drawing France into the strategic alliance than the Declaration of Independence was.

The rest of Europe was similarly silent, although many newspapers printed full translations of the document. Official mentions are few and far between. Even the Count of Aranda, the Spanish representative in France—an admirer of Franklin and Jefferson and an advocate of Spain joining the war on the Americans' behalf—was conspicuously silent in

The Marquis de Lafayette, who wrote an early draft of the *Declaration of the Rights of Man and Citizen*, was known to be an admirer of the Declaration of Independence.

his official dispatches home. European intellectuals took a detached approach to the Declaration of Independence. Although the American statement was intellectually interesting, its radical republicanism was at odds with European traditionalism. Liberal Europeans of the period (for example, in France or the German states) were not seeking to overthrow their monarchies, but rather to guarantee individual rights within the existing system.

The Declaration of the Rights of Man and Citizen owes little to the Declaration of Independence. More like a Bill of Rights, it enumerates the fundamental rights of the French citizenry.

The first translations of the Declaration of Independence into French appeared in journals outside the country—it was not until after the 1778 alliance that the text of the Declaration of Independence was published in France. One of the earliest translators was the Duc de La Rochefoucauld d'Enville, a friend of Benjamin Franklin, and Franklin himself is said to have assisted with the task. La Rochefoucauld, a delegate to the Assemblée Nationale, was an admirer of the Declaration of Independence, as was the Marquis de Lafayette, who wrote an early draft of the *Declaration of the Rights of Man and Citizen*, adopted by the Assemblée Nationale in 1789 and incorporated into the constitution in 1791.

Many French politicians were aware of the Declaration of Independence as they were drafting their own declaration, and were known to have consulted with both Benjamin Franklin and Thomas Jefferson, yet the French declaration has more in common with the various state constitutions and Bills of Rights; the Assemblée had copies of these documents as well, and both the Virginia Bill of Rights and the Pennsylvania constitution were held in high regard. Although the Assemblée was known to have consulted the American documents throughout their two-year-long debate, there are few echoes of the American texts in the French document. In large part, this has to do with the different purposes of the two declarations: whereas the Americans were declaring their independence and breaking free of an oppressive ruler, the French were trying the educate the populace about their rights in the face of the continuing existence of the absolute monarchy, in an attempt to limit abuses of power in the future.

Simon Bolivar and Francisco de Miranda sign the Venezuelan Declaration of Independence against Spanish rule on July 5, 1811. Although the American Revolution inspired insurgency movements in New Spain, the text of the Declaration of Independence itself had little influence.

Although the French declaration enumerates the rights of the French people, they have only the slimmest resemblance to Jefferson's "life, liberty, and the pursuit of happiness": among the "natural, unalienable, and secure rights" in the French document are "liberty, security, property, and resistance to oppression." It then goes on to list other rights, including the right to free speech and freedom of the press, and asserts the ultimate sovereignty of the people, more in the spirit of a Bill of Rights than the Declaration of Independence.

The Nineteenth and Twentieth Centuries
During the nineteenth century, revolutionary movements, although they may have taken to heart the sentiments

expressed in the Declaration, made little use of the document. The aims of revolutions in Germany and Russia, for example, were not to break free of a colonial power, but rather to revise their forms of government. Radicals were more interested in practical documents, especially the national and state constitutions.

New Spain (Mexico), which was seeking independence from colonial rule, also ignored the Declaration of Independence, although it was published in books and newspapers in Mexico during the 1810s, and the American Revolution was held up as an inspiration for the New World. However, Jefferson's language, so revolutionary in its time, was not applied to the Mexican bid for independence. This may in part have been caused by a measure of resentment: the U.S. government had refused aid to the Mexican insurgents, fearful that it would bring Spain into the War of 1812 on the side of Britain. Also, the revolution in the Spanish American colonies took a far different course. In the end the emancipation of New Spain was achieved peacefully, as Spain recognized the impossibility of controlling so extensive an empire.

In nineteenth-century Japan, on the other hand, the Declaration of Independence was very influential among radical groups and even established politicians, as they rewrote their own constitution and aimed to reform their society. The Declaration was first published in Japan during the 1860s, after the first U.S.–Japan treaty in 1854 raised

During the Meiji Enlightenment in the nineteenth century, Japan opened up to foreign influences. This print of 1873 by Hiroshige III is one example: two foreigners ride horses, in front of newly installed telegraph wires, against an otherwise traditional backdrop of Mount Fuji. The Declaration of Independence was first published in Japan in the 1860s.

Japan's new constitution, written by the Americans under General Douglas MacArthur (above), used phrasing taken directly from the Declaration of Independence, as well as other seminal documents.

awareness of American culture. This coincided with a period of Japanese history known as the Meiji Enlightenment, a time of modernization and the opening up of Japanese culture to influences from around the world. The Declaration was widely read and greatly respected for its assertions of liberty and equality. Mainstream publications held the Declaration of Independence up as an inspirational document as Japan revised its constitution, even though it was not seeking to establish a republic. The Declaration also became a central text of the radical people's rights movement, which sought to break down established class and economic barriers in Japanese society.

During the twentieth century the Declaration of Independence returned to prominence in Japan, this time during the American occupation following World War II. As part of his efforts to "rehabilitate" Japan, General Douglas MacArthur planned to introduce a new Japanese constitution to replace the Meiji Constitution. MacArthur's version would dramatically limit the power of the emperor, effectively reducing him to a figurehead.

The new constitution, as drafted by a committee of lawyers and officers at MacArthur's headquarters, contains words and phrases not only from the Declaration of Independence, but also from the Constitution, the Bill of Rights, and the Gettysburg Address. These allusions leap out in a reading of the preamble:

We, the Japanese People, acting through our duly elected representatives in the National Diet . . . do proclaim the sovereignty of the people's will and do ordain and establish this Constitution, founded upon the universal principle that government is a sacred trust the authority for which is derived from the people, the powers of which are exercised by the representatives of the people, and the benefits of which are enjoyed by the people.

Later in the document, among the guarantees in the extensive Bill of Rights section is the "right to life, liberty, and the pursuit of happiness." Just as the Declaration of Independence was influential in the drafting of the Meiji Constitution, so its ideas lived on in the 1946 version. This time, however, the American authorities also incorporated echoes of the French *Declaration of the Rights of Man*, the Soviet Constitution of 1918, and the Weimar Constitution of 1919.

During the twentieth century the language of the Declaration of Independence also returned to the forefront of revolutionary movements, when Ho Chi Minh included it in his own declaration of independence for the Vietnamese people on September 2, 1945, announcing the establishment of an independent republic in North Vietnam, with its capital in Hanoi. Ho Chi Minh was the founder and leader of the Viet Minh, which aimed to free Vietnam from Japanese and French occupation and unify the country. Widely traveled and broadly read, he was also an operative for the U.S. Office of

Ho Chi Minh, the Vietnamese communist leader and first president of North Vietnam, cited the Declaration of Independence in his own declaration of independence for the Vietnamese people in 1945.

Strategic Services (the precursor of the CIA), and it is known that he checked his quotations from the Declaration of Independence with a fellow operative, an American, before delivering his own version. It begins with a direct quote:

"All men are created equal. They are endowed by their Creator with certain unalienable rights, among these are Life, Liberty, and the pursuit of Happiness."
This immortal statement was made in the Declaration of Independence of the United States of America in 1776. In a broader sense, this means: All the peoples on the earth are equal from birth, all the peoples have a right to live, to be happy and free.

Ho Chi Minh subtly altered Jefferson's words when he translated the text: the word he uses for "men" in the first quotation was rendered in Vietnamese with a word that actually translates back as "people." In this way, and in the interpretation he offers in the following sentences, Ho Chi Minh was making Jefferson's message explicitly inclusive, offering equality and equal rights to women as well as men.

Ho Chi Minh also echoed the structure of the Declaration of Independence. He begins with a preamble, which mentions and quotes from the French *Declaration of the Rights of Man*—especially significant since Vietnam was at the time a French colonial possession. Just as with the Declaration of Independence, the preamble is followed by a list of grievances. At first they are generic, each beginning with the word "they"—just as Jefferson began the American charges with "he." Later, however, Ho Chi Minh departs from this rhythm, making his accusations far more specific and detailed. The closing also alludes to the Declaration of Independence:

> For these reasons, we, members of the Provisional Government of the Democratic Republic of Vietnam, solemnly declare to the world that Vietnam has the right to be a free and independent country—and in fact it is so already. The entire Vietnamese people are determined to mobilize all their physical and mental strength, to sacrifice their lives and property in order to safeguard their independence and liberty.

In the light of the Vietnam War, it is ironic that Ho Chi Minh based his establishment of the Vietnamese republic on this quintessentially American document.

UNDERSTANDING THE DECLARATION OF INDEPENDENCE
AFTERMATH

I have a dream that one day this nation will rise up and live out the true meaning of the creed: "We hold these truths to be self-evident that all men are created equal."

Martin Luther King Jr., August 28, 1963

The War of 1812, between the United States and Great Britain, was the culmination of more than ten years of tension between the two countries, evidenced by a series of trade embargoes and British threats to American shipping. The course of the war was not favorable to the Americans. Much of the American navy was blockaded in harbor by the superior British fleet, and British forces reached as far south as Washington, D.C., burning the White House and forcing the president to flee, before being routed at Baltimore. Yet late military progress by the Americans, as well as ongoing diplomacy, which began as soon as the war did, meant that it ended in a stalemate. The terms of the 1815 Treaty of Ghent were a source of American pride, because the British did not achieve their aims: control of the Great Lakes and the creation of a Native American state under their control. Rather, a boundary commission was established to formalize the Canadian border based on territory held before the beginning of the war. That said, the Americans did not achieve their aims either, since the tricky issues of the impressment of American sailors and the enforcement of the rights of neutral nations were never on the table.

The war's end in 1815 marked a sea change in the American consciousness, with the development of a new

feeling of nationalism. Although the Americans did not win the war, they did not lose either. They held their own in an international conflict and won some memorable victories. Andrew Jackson's famous victory at New Orleans on January 15, 1815, although taking place two weeks after the Treaty of Ghent officially ended hostilities, nonetheless stirred up patriotic fervor. This was heightened as rapid industrialization in the early 1820s brought unprecedented prosperity across the country.

As part of this new feeling of national pride, Americans began reexamining their own history. During the decades leading up to the 50th anniversary of the Declaration of Independence in 1826, major books treating American history, such as Mercy Otis Warren's three-volume *History of the American Revolution* (1805), came out. The public was newly curious about the early days of the American republic and the patriots who won independence from Great Britain. Biographies of the signers of the Declaration of Independence were published in droves.

Thomas Jefferson's role as draftsman of the Declaration made him a focus of historical interest and enquiry. He estimated in the early 1820s that he responded to about a thousand letters each year, many of which related to queries about the early history of the United States, and in particular the revolutionary era. John Adams was also a prolific correspondent, who greatly resented Jefferson's high profile, and he too engaged in extensive correspondence with keen historians. Letters also traveled

Top: **Andrew Jackson won a famous victory at New Orleans that contributed to the revival of American patriotism. Here he is memorialized in a statue in the city's French Quarter.**

Above: **the Battle of New Orleans was fought two weeks after the war of 1812 had officially ended with the Treaty of Ghent.**

John Trumbull's grand painting of the signing of the Declaration of Independence was unveiled in 1818. Today, it is one of the most famous depictions of the events of the revolutionary period.

frequently between the two men, with each man supporting his own particular version of early American history at the same time as together they lamented the deaths of their former colleagues.

Images relating to the early history of the United States also became popular. Various facsimiles of the Declaration of Independence (including those made directly from the actual embossed, parchment version) were marketed to eager buyers celebrating the nation's history. John Trumbull's large painting of the signing of the Declaration of Independence was unveiled in the Rotunda of the new Capitol building in 1818. Jefferson had suggested the idea of painting the scene to Trumbull in 1787 when both men were in Paris, and then furnished him with a sketch of the Assembly Room in the Old Pennsylvania State House (today known as Independence Hall). Jefferson's recollections were not entirely accurate, and the painting contains several architectural inaccuracies that were incorporated into a smaller painting completed in 1793 as well as the larger work.

After 1815, July 4 evolved into a major celebration: it was around this time that the tradition of reading out the Declaration of Independence on July 4 came about, and the Declaration became a well-known and well-loved document. The date was often selected to launch significant projects, such as the building of the Ohio Canal or the Baltimore and Ohio Railroad.

In 1819 a scandal broke out over the Mecklenburg Declaration of Independence, a document claiming to be a precursor to the national Declaration. On April 30 that year a North Carolina paper, the *Raleigh Register*, published a story about the so-called Mecklenburg Declaration of Independence, said to have been adopted by the North Carolina Convention on May 20, 1775, the day after news of the battle of Lexington reached them. Although neither the actual document nor the minutes of the meeting survived, the Mecklenburg Declaration was recreated by Joseph McKnitt Alexander, from notes that were kept by his father, John McKnitt Alexander, the clerk of the Convention.

Similarity in language between the Mecklenburg Declaration and Jefferson's text caused quite a stir. For example, the Mecklenburg document asserts the "inherent and inalienable rights of man"; radically it also dissolves the "political bands" between England and America. Had the Mecklenburg declaration been authentic, Jefferson's declaration—the national one—would have lost some of its mystique and Jefferson's achievement, now so celebrated, would have appeared diminished. In his correspondence, Jefferson vehemently denied any prior knowledge of the Mecklenburg Declaration, calling it "spurious." Today most historians doubt the veracity of the Mecklenburg Declaration, yet it still has its advocates in North Carolina, the state that rightly claims to be "first in freedom" because it was the first to instruct its delegates to the Continental Congress to vote for independence.

Fifty years after the signing of the Declaration of Independence, the lives of two of the founding fathers—Thomas Jefferson and John Adams—came to an end. Jefferson lapsed into a coma on the night of July 3, 1826, but held on until the following noon; his last words were reported as, "Is it the Fourth?" At nearly the same moment as his old friend died, Adams, sitting in his armchair and reading, collapsed into unconsciousness. He died five hours later, with the words "Jefferson still lives" said to be his last.

Women's Rights

As the Declaration of Independence became part of the American consciousness, its words—specifically the promises made in the preamble—were taken up by groups fighting for equality.

The women's suffrage movement used the text of the Declaration of Independence when it issued its Declaration of Sentiments following the Seneca Falls Convention in July 1848. More than 300 delegates, both men and women, attended this first-ever women's rights convention and signed the Declaration, which was written by Elizabeth Cady Stanton.

The Declaration of Sentiments self-consciously used the Declaration of Independence as a template. Like its precursor, it is in three parts: the preamble is virtually identical, although it uses more inclusive language:

When, in the course of human events, it becomes necessary for one portion of the family of man to

Elizabeth Cady Stanton (seated here alongside Susan B. Anthony), modeled the Declaration of Sentiments, issued by the Seneca Falls Convention, on the Declaration of Independence. It was signed by more than 300 delegates to the first women's rights convention.

assume among the people of the earth a position
different from that which they have hitherto occupied,
but one to which the laws of nature and of nature's
God entitle them, a decent respect to the opinions of
mankind requires that they should declare the causes
that impel them to such a course.
We hold these truths to be self-evident: that all
men and women are created equal; that they are
endowed by their Creator with certain inalienable
rights; that among these are life, liberty, and the pursuit
of happiness; that to secure these rights governments
are instituted, deriving their just powers from the
consent of the governed.

Finally, the Seneca Falls Declaration makes itself perfectly clear: "The history of mankind is a history of repeated injuries and usurpations on the part of man toward woman, having in direct object the establishment of an absolute tyranny over her. To prove this, let facts be submitted to a candid world." It then goes on to present its grievances against the male establishment, which are summed up in 15 quite specific charges, ranging from the matter-of-fact ("He has never permitted her to exercise her inalienable right to the elective franchise; He has compelled her to submit to laws, in the formation of which she had no voice") to the more emotive ("He has endeavored, in every way that he could, to destroy her confidence in her own powers, to lessen her self-respect and to make her willing to lead a dependent and abject life"). It concludes with a series of resolutions that established the long-term goals for the women's rights movement—some of which have still not been attained.

Like the Declaration of Independence before it, the Seneca Falls Declaration had few tangible results. Although it was widely publicized, it met with a mixed reception and was mocked by most male commentators in the mainstream press. However, like the Declaration of Independence, it also came to play a role as a source of inspiration for the movement, even to this day.

Elizabeth Cady Stanton and Lucretia Mott, who jointly organized the Seneca Falls Convention, had met eight years earlier at the World Anti-Slavery Convention in London, where as women they had been refused the right to speak, even though they were official delegates. In terms of membership and ideals, there was a great deal of crossover between the suffrage movement and the abolitionist movement—many women became committed to the fight for their own rights after participating on an equal footing with men in the abolitionist movement.

Abolition

David Walker, writing in *Walker's Appeal*, 1823, said:

> *See your Declaration Americans!!! Do you understand your own language? Hear your languages, proclaimed to the world, July 4th, 1776—"We hold these truths to be self evident—that ALL MEN ARE CREATED EQUAL!! that they* are endowed by their Creator with certain

White Lady, happy, proud and free,
Lend awhile thine ear to me ;
Let the Negro Mother's wail
Turn thy pale cheek still more pale.
Can the Negro Mother joy
Over this her captive boy,
Which in bondage and in tears,
For a life of wo she rears ?
Though she bears a Mother's name,
A Mother's rights she may not claim ;
For the white man's will can part,
Her darling from her bursting heart.

From the Genius of Universal Emancipation.
LETTERS ON SLAVERY.—No. III.

Close ties between suffrage and abolition are illustrated in this page from *The Liberator*, the leading abolitionist newspaper. This poem appealed to women to join the abolitionist movement.

unalienable rights*; that among these are life,* liberty, *and the pursuit of happiness!!" Compare your own language above, extracted from your Declaration of Independence, with your cruelties and murders inflicted by your cruel and unmerciful fathers and yourselves on our fathers and on us—men who have never given your fathers or you the least provocation!!!!!!*

Slavery had always been a contentious issue in American life and politics. Jefferson, himself a slave owner, had included involvement in the slave trade among the charges against King George III, but Congress had deleted this section, preferring to leave the issue aside altogether. In his own time Jefferson felt no conflict between slavery and asserting that "all men are created equal," since he was using the term in a very narrow, philosophical sense that he believed all his contemporaries understood.

However, even in the early days of American independence, the argument of the Declaration of Independence resounded with those opposed to slavery. Consider the first few lines of this petition arguing for the abolition of slavery, signed by 19 slaves in New Hampshire and presented to the state assembly:

The petition of the subscribers, natives of Africa, now forcibly detained in slavery in said state most humbly sheweth. That the God of nature gave them life and freedom, upon the terms of the most perfect equality with other men; That freedom is an inherent right of the human species, not to be surrendered, but by consent, for the sake of social life; That private or public tyranny and slavery are alike detestable to minds conscious of the equal dignity of human nature.

Its argument runs parallel to that of the Declaration of Independence, using very similar phrasing.

From the 1820s, the language of the Declaration of Independence, and the promises inherent in it, were taken

up to great rhetorical effect by the abolitionist movement in the fight against slavery. Numerous articles in pamphlets and journals took issue with the continuing practice of slavery, pointing out the conflict between the spirit of the founding document of the United States and the "peculiar institution." Abolitionists argued their cause on moral grounds, returning to the idea of natural law advocated by Jefferson in the Declaration of Independence, and held up that document in support of their cause.

This 1835 lithograph depicts an early abolitionist meeting in Boston, during which William Lloyd Garrison was attacked by a mob and dragged through the streets with a rope around his neck; he was finally rescued by the mayor, who placed him in the city jail for safety.

To William Lloyd Garrison, abolitionist and founder of *The Liberator*, the leading abolitionist newspaper, the Declaration of Independence and abolition were inextricably linked. "I am a believer in that portion of the Declaration of American Independence in which it is set forth, as among self-evident truths, 'that all men are created equal; that they are endowed by their Creator with certain inalienable rights; that among these are life, liberty, and the pursuit of happiness.' Hence, I am an abolitionist."

Garrison often used the words of the Declaration in his powerful arguments against slavery. The Declaration of

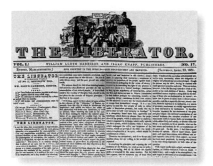

Independence played a prominent role in the Declaration of Sentiments of the American Anti-Slavery Convention, written by Garrison in 1833. In this document he not only evokes the word of the Declaration, but also places the abolition of slavery in a historical continuum, relating it directly to the winning of independence half a century beforehand:

More than fifty-seven years have elapsed, since a band of patriots convened in this place, to devise measures for the deliverance of this country from a foreign yoke. The corner-stone upon which they founded the Temple of Freedom was broadly this— "that all men are created equal; that they are endowed by their Creator with certain inalienable rights; that among these are life, LIBERTY, and the pursuit of happiness." At the sound of their trumpet-call, three millions of people rose up as from the sleep of death, and rushed to the strife of blood; deeming it more glorious to die instantly as freemen, than desirable to live one hour as slaves. They were few in number—poor in resource; but the honest conviction that Truth, Justice and Right were on their side, made them invincible.

We have met together for the achievement of an enterprise, without which that of our fathers is incomplete; and which, for its magnitude, solemnity, and probable results upon the destiny of the world, as far transcends theirs as moral truth does physical force.

The former president, John Quincy Adams, was already well known for his anti-slavery views when he took on the case of the African mutineers from the *Amistad*. His eloquent defense won them their freedom and the right to return home to Africa.

The Supreme Court

The Supreme Court has turned to the moral force of the Declaration of Independence for guidance in more than 100 cases over the years, and most of these cases involve civil rights issues. The Amistad case was the first in which the Declaration was summoned up to demonstrate the underlying ethos of the country.

In February 1839, two Portuguese slave traders illegally captured and transported a large group of people from Sierra Leone to the slave market in Cuba, where 53 of the men and women were purchased by two Spanish planters. While sailing on the *Amistad* to Cuba, the Africans seized control of the ship on July 1 and murdered the captain and the cook, sparing the two Spaniards, whom they ordered to sail the ship back to Africa. Instead the Spaniards directed the ship eastward, and on August 24 it was taken by the U.S. brigantine *Washington*. The Africans were imprisoned in New Haven, Connecticut, charged with murder, and the Spanish planters were freed. Although the murder charge was soon dismissed, the Africans continued to be held in prison while their future was debated. The argument turned on the concept of property rights: Were they Spanish property and thus liable to extradition to Cuba, as the Spanish government proposed, to face trial on mutiny and murder charges? Or were they human beings, and thus free now that they were cleared of murder?

After the Connecticut district court ruled that they should be returned to Africa as free men and women,

This portrait of Joseph Cinque, the leader of the revolt on the *Amistad*, was offered for sale by the *New York Sun* during the trial. The text below quotes Cinque's speech, delivered to his compatriots on board ship after the mutiny: "Brothers, we have done that which we purposed, our hands are now clean for we have striven to regain the precious heritage we received from our fathers . . . I am resolved it is better to die than to be a white man's slave . . ."

President Martin Van Buren, at the behest of the Spanish government and not willing to lose support in the southern slave states, referred the case to the U.S. Supreme Court. The Africans' lawyer, Roger Baldwin, the grandson of a signer of the Declaration of Independence, asked John Quincy Adams to make their case to the Supreme Court.

Adams (the son of John Adams) was 73 years old in 1841, when the *Amistad* case was finally heard by the Supreme Court. After an undistinguished term as U.S. president, he entered the House of Representatives in 1831, where he made a name for himself as an anti-slavery activist. He was deeply moved by the plight of the Africans, but found the *Amistad* case difficult to frame because of the absence of any legal precedent on which he could base his argument.

Ultimately Adams returned to fundamentals. As he said in his argument, which lasted more than eight hours and was heard over two days: "I know of no other law that reaches the case of my clients, but the law of Nature and of Nature's God on which our fathers placed our own existence." And he used the Declaration of Independence to give his argument moral force: "Is it possible to speak of this demand [to extradite the Africans to Cuba] in the language of decency and moderation? . . . Has the expunging process of black lines passed up these two Declarations of Independence in their gilded frames? Has the 4th of July '76 become a day of ignomiy and reproach?"

Although the case was specifically based on property rights, Adams extended his argument to dispute the legitimacy of the institution of slavery itself. He maintained that the Declaration of Independence showed that the case was closed. "The moment you come to the Declaration of Independence, that every man has a right to life and liberty, an inalienable right, this case is decided. I ask nothing more on behalf of these unfortunate men than this Declaration."

The Supreme Court took a month to reach its decision, written by Judge Joseph Story, which established that human beings were not property and thus the Africans were free. Eventually the 35 Africans who survived the *Amistad* and the Connecticut prison returned to Sierra Leone, after money was raised through private charitable donations to fund their journey home.

The Dred Scott case reached the Supreme Court in 1856. As the personal slave to a U.S. army surgeon, Scott had left Missouri, a slave state, and gone to live in Illinois, a free state, and then the Wisconsin territory (also free). After his master's death, he sued his master's family to win freedom for himself and his own family on the grounds that their residency in a free state had ended his bondage. The Supreme Court was split by the case, reluctant to declare the Missouri Compromise unconstitutional, although it ruled against Scott in the decision written by Chief Justice Roger B. Taney.

In the opinion of the court, the laws of Illinois no longer applied to a resident of Missouri, and thus his bondage was not negated. Even more significantly, it maintained that as a black man, he could not be a citizen of the United States and thus had no recourse to sue in the federal courts. In his decision, Taney referred to the claims of abolitionists that slavery was not in line with the promises inherent in the Declaration of Independence, when he wrote: "[I]t is too clear for dispute, that the enslaved African race were not intended to be included, and formed no part of the people who framed and adopted this Declaration." Dissenting Supreme Court justices wrote their own opinions, disputing the judgment on all grounds, yet the case stood.

Abraham Lincoln and the Declaration of Independence
Abraham Lincoln, at the time a rising politician, vehemently targeted the Dred Scott decision. To him, it represented not only the antithesis of his own political creed, but a betrayal of what America stood for. He deeply respected the founding fathers and gained inspiration from the words of the Declaration of Independence. As he said after being elected president in 1861: "[A]ll the political sentiments I entertain have been drawn, so far as I have been able to draw them, from the sentiments which originated and were given to the world from this hall. I have never had a feeling politically that did not spring from the sentiments embodied in the Declaration of Independence.

Lincoln took to heart the attacks on the Declaration made by the supporters of slavery, such as Senator John C. Calhoun of South Carolina, who maintained that there "was not a word of truth" in the Declaration's assertions of human

Abraham Lincoln delivers a speech on February 2, 1861, at a flag raising at Independence Hall, Philadelphia. Lincoln had stopped there on his way to Washington, D.C., for his inauguration. His off-the-cuff speech reaffirmed his belief in the promises made by the Declaration of Independence.

equality, and that such phrases were included in error in the famous text. He took issue with such claims, as well as with other contentious issues. For example, in a famous speech in Chicago in June 1857, Lincoln directly addressed the issue that still troubles many contemporary readers of the Declaration of Independence: that a document that promises freedom to all was written and signed by slave owners:

> I think the authors of that notable instrument intended to include all men, but they did not intend to declare all men equal in all respects. They did not mean to say all were equal in color, size, intellect, moral developments, or social capacity. They defined with tolerable distinctness, in what respects they did consider all men created equal—equal in "certain inalienable rights, among which are life, liberty, and the pursuit of happiness." This they said, and this meant.
> They did not mean to assert the obvious untruth, that all were then actually enjoying that equality, nor yet, that they were about to confer it immediately upon them. In fact they had no power to confer such a boon. They meant simply to declare the right, so that the enforcement of it might follow as fast as circumstances should permit. They meant to set up a standard maxim for free society, which should be familiar to all, and revered by all; constantly looked to, constantly labored for, and even though never perfectly attained,

constantly approximated, and thereby constantly spreading and deepening its influence, and augmenting the happiness and value of life to all people of all colors everywhere.

To Lincoln, the Declaration of Independence established the ultimate goal of a just society—that all members of that society should attain the rights it set forth. It was also a universal document, in its inclusive spirit applicable anywhere and to any people.

Lincoln's broad interpretation of the Declaration of Independence became one focus of the famous debates with Stephen A. Douglas, a rival for the Senate seat for Illinois in 1858. Douglas was a prominent politician, in Congress since 1843 and seeking his third term as senator. He was a leading Democrat, although a divisive figure within the party. His policy of "popular sovereignty," or leaving the decision on slavery to the state level, had led him to oppose national Democratic politics on more than one occasion. Lincoln, on the other hand, was new to national politics and had slim hope of actually winning the election.

Douglas's high profile meant that the campaign received national coverage. Although senators were at the time elected by state legislators rather than by popular vote (a practice that continued until 1913), Douglas and Lincoln took their campaigns to the people, traveling across the state and addressing large crowds. Lincoln also challenged Douglas to seven debates, a challenge to which Douglas reluctantly agreed. These debates came to be about much more than the Senate seat—the two were debating the future of slavery, and in fact the future of the United States itself.

The Declaration of Independence, so often cited by Lincoln, was disputed by the two men, each trying to claim the text for his own cause. Douglas contested Lincoln's assertion that the Declaration of Independence guaranteed equal rights to blacks as well as whites:

I tell you that this Chicago doctrine of Lincoln's—declaring that the negro and the white man are made equal by the Declaration of Independence and by Divine Providence—is a monstrous heresy. The signers of the Declaration of Independence never dreamed of the negro when they were writing that document. They referred to white men, to men of European birth and European descent, when they declared the equality of all men . . . When that Declaration was put forth every one of the thirteen colonies were slaveholding colonies, and every man who signed that instrument represented a slaveholding constituency. Recollect, also, that no one of them emancipated his slaves, much less put them on an equality with himself, after he signed the Declaration. On the contrary, they all continued to hold their negroes as slaves during the revolutionary war . . . When you say that the Declaration of Independence includes the negro, you charge the signers of it with hypocrisy.

This statue of Stephen A. Douglas, senator from Illinois from 1847 to 1861, stands outside the Illinois State Capitol building. The debates between Lincoln and Douglas during the presidential campaign of 1860 often concerned their varying interpretations of the Declaration of Independence.

I say to you, frankly, that in my opinion this government was made by our fathers on the white basis. It was made by white men for the benefit of white men and their posterity forever, and was intended to be administered by white men in all time to come.

And Lincoln responded:

I believe the entire records of the world, from the date of the Declaration of Independence up to within three years ago, may be searched in vain for one single affirmation, from one single man, that the negro was not included in the Declaration of Independence. I think I may defy Judge Douglas to show that he ever said so, that Washington ever said so, that any President ever said so, that any member of Congress ever said so . . . And I will remind Judge Douglas and this audience, that while Mr. Jefferson was the owner of slaves, as undoubtedly he was, in speaking upon this very subject, he used the strong language that "he trembled for his country when he remembered that God was just."

Although Lincoln eventually lost the election, the campaign established him as a major political figure and irreparably weakened Douglas's support within his own party. Lincoln's victory over Douglas in the presidential election of 1860 was a direct result of this. Throughout his political life Lincoln made frequent recourse to the Declaration; his citations of it gave that historic document a new and lasting resonance, and it became the defining doctrine of American life.

Martin Luther King, Jr., speaks from the Lincoln Memorial to crowds gathered for the march on Washington in August 1963, delivering his "I have a dream . . ." speech.

In an off-the-cuff speech in the Old State House in Philadelphia at the time of his first inauguration as president, Lincoln talked about the primacy of the promises made in the Declaration of Independence:

I have often inquired of myself what great principle or idea it was that kept this Confederacy so long together. It was not the mere matter of the separation of the Colonies from the motherland; but that sentiment in the Declaration of Independence which gave liberty, not alone to the people of this country, but, I hope, to the world, for all future time. It was that which gave promise that in due time the weight would be lifted from the shoulders of all men. This is a sentiment embodied in the Declaration of Independence.

Now, my friends, can this country be saved upon that basis? If it can, I will consider myself one of the happiest men in the world, if I can help to save it. If it cannot be saved upon that principle, it will be truly awful. But if this country cannot be saved without giving up that principle, I was about to say I would rather be assassinated on this spot than surrender it.

"I have a dream"

Abraham Lincoln believed that the Declaration of Independence offered up an "abstract truth, applicable to all men and all times." And its continuing use as a rallying cry for civil rights progress has proved him right.

The founding spirit of America was again summoned by Martin Luther King, Jr., in the most famous speech of his career, and perhaps the most memorable address of the civil rights movement. Fittingly, it was delivered at the Lincoln Memorial, at the culmination of the march on Washington in August 1963, 100 years after the Gettysburg Address and the Emancipation Proclamation that freed all slaves:

And so we've come here today to dramatize a shameful condition. In a sense, we've come to our nation's capital to cash a check. When the architects of our republic wrote the magnificent words of the Constitution and the Declaration of Independence, they were signing a promissory note to which every American was to fall heir. This note was a promise that all men, yes, black men as well as white men, would be guaranteed the unalienable rights of "Life, Liberty and the pursuit of Happiness."

It is obvious today that America has defaulted on this promissory note insofar as her citizens of color are concerned. Instead of honoring this sacred obligation, America has given the Negro people a bad check, a check which has come back marked "insufficient funds." But we refuse to believe that the bank of justice is bankrupt. We refuse to believe that there are insufficient funds in the great vaults of opportunity of this nation. So we've come to cash this check, a check that will give us upon demand the riches of freedom and the security of justice.

I have a dream that one day this nation will rise up and live out the true meaning of the creed: "We hold these truths to be self-evident that all men are created equal."

King's dream was beyond the range of what Lincoln imagined possible—and well beyond the range of Jefferson's imagination. Today the Declaration of Independence remains at the heart of civil rights debates: for example, both supporters and opponents of affirmative action cite the text of the Declaration of Independence in support of their positions. In its boundless scope, it is a distinctively American document.

A Charter of Freedom

The Declaration of Independence lives on not only in spirit but also as a physical document. It escaped damage during the Revolution as it traveled from one safe haven to another with Congress. When the Capitol burned during the War of 1812, it was safely ensconced in a private home in Leesburg, Virginia. During World War II it was safeguarded in Fort Knox.

Although it was saved from disaster time and again, it was not preserved from the ravages of time. By the time it was 50 years old, the Declaration was already reported to be in quite rough condition, both because it had been much handled and because copies had repeatedly been made using a "wet transfer" process that diluted the ink and weakened the parchment. By its centennial in 1876, the Declaration was in terrible condition, faded and crumbling.

When the Capitol and the White House were burned by the British during the War of 1812, the Declaration of Independence was safely stored in a private home in Leesburg, Virginia, saving it from destruction.

The Liberty Bell, so named because it rang on July 8, 1776, to announce the first public reading of the Declaration of Independence, is on display in Independence National Historic Park in Philadelphia, Pennsylvania.

Although it was finally encased in a sturdy frame, protected from handling, it was still exposed to sunlight, which caused further deterioration.

In 1952, with great ceremony, it was encased in a box made of glass treated with gelatine to control light exposure and filled with helium to prevent oxidation. This was put on display in the Library of Congress. There it stayed until 2001, when it was carefully removed to undergo a two-year conservation process. The parchment was humidified to remove small lumps, known as cockles, that had developed over the years. Then each letter was scanned with a microscope to spot any loose flakes of ink. Each flake was replaced using tiny drops of special adhesive, and damage to the parchment was repaired using a special Japanese paper.

Today the embossed manuscript copy of the Declaration of Independence is housed in the National Archives in Washington, D.C. Alongside the Constitution and the Bill of Rights, it is displayed to the public in a titanium frame, under a rotunda dome designed by John Russell Pope, also the architect of the Jefferson Memorial.

Historical Sites

The Pennsylvania State House, where the Declaration of Independence was debated and signed by the Continental Congress, is today known as Independence Hall and is a UNESCO World Heritage Site. It is preserved as part of the Independence National Historical Park in Philadelphia, also home to the Liberty Bell, which rang on July 8, 1776, to

To celebrate the 225th anniversary of the Declaration, television producer Norman Lear organized the Declaration of Independence Roadtrip, a non-profit, non-partisan project, with the goal of taking the document to the people. A Dunlap Broadside, owned by Lear, traveled cross-country from July 2001 to November 2004, visiting towns and cities across the nation and inspiring civic activism, especially among today's young Americans.

announce the first public reading of the Declaration of Independence. Graff House (today known as Declaration House), where Jefferson lodged while he drafted the Declaration of Independence, is also part of the national park complex. There Jefferson's swivel chair and the lap desk he reputedly used while writing are on display.

Thomas Jefferson believed that his drafting of the Declaration was one of his life's crowning achievements. When he wrote the epitaph that he wished to appear on his tombstone, he offered the following words: "Author of the Declaration of American Independence, of the State of Virginia for Religious Freedom, and Father of the University of Virginia."

His authorship of the Declaration of Independence is further memorialized in the Jefferson Memorial in Washington, D.C. President Franklin Delano Roosevelt suggested the idea of a memorial to Jefferson, with the aim of generating a patriotic spirit and garnering support for World War II. Congress duly authorized a commission to plan and build a memorial to Jefferson in 1934. There was controversy within the architectural community, because the selection process was not subject to open competition. The honor of designing the memorial went to John Russell Pope, and he based it on the dome of the Pantheon in Rome—an architectural element that Jefferson used both for his home, Monticello, and for the University of Virginia. Inside the dome is a massive bronze statue of Jefferson, standing and staring out toward the White House. Among the inscriptions on the statue base and around the chamber is a much-edited quotation from the Declaration of Independence.

We hold these truths to be self-evident that all men are created equal, that they are endowed by their Creator with certain unalienable rights, among these are life, liberty, and the pursuit of happiness, that to secure these rights governments are instituted among men. We . . . solemnly publish and declare, that these colonies are and of right ought to be free and independent states . . . And for the support of this declaration, with a firm reliance on the protection of divine providence, we mutually pledge our lives, our fortunes, and our sacred honor.

This quotation reflects less the historical necessities that inspired the drafting of the Declaration than it does our contemporary interpretation. But that in itself proves an important point. The Declaration of Independence remains a living document, open to debate and interpretation even today.

THOMAS JEFFERSON'S ROUGH DRAFT OF THE DECLARATION OF INDEPENDENCE

A Declaration By the Representatives of the United States of America, in General Congress Assembled.

When in the course of human events it becomes necessary for a people to advance from that subordination in which they have hitherto remained, and to assume among powers of the earth the equal and independent station to which the laws of nature and of nature's god entitle them, a decent respect to the opinions of mankind requires that they should declare the causes which impel them to the change.

We hold these truths to be self-evident; that all men are created equal and independent; that from that equal creation they derive rights inherent and inalienable, among which are the preservation of life, and liberty, and the pursuit of happiness; that to secure these ends, governments are instituted among men, deriving their just power from the consent of the governed; that whenever any form of government shall become destructive of these ends, it is the right of the people to alter or to abolish it, and to institute new government, laying its foundation on such principles and organizing its power in such form, as to them shall seem most likely to effect their safety and happiness. Prudence indeed will dictate that governments long established should not be changed for light and transient causes: and accordingly all experience hath shewn that mankind are more disposed to suffer while evils are sufferable, than to right themselves by abolishing the forms to which they are accustomed. But when a long train of abuses and usurpations, begun at a distinguished period, and pursuing invariably the same object, evinces a design to reduce them to arbitrary power, it is their right, it is their duty, to throw off such government and to provide new guards for future security. Such has been the patient sufferings of the colonies; and such is now the necessity which constrains them to expunge their former systems of government. The history of his present majesty is a history of unremitting injuries and usurpations, among which no one fact stands single or solitary to contradict the uniform tenor of the rest, all of which have in direct object the establishment of an absolute tyranny over these states. To prove this, let facts be submitted to a candid world, for the truth of which we pledge a faith yet unsullied by falsehood.

He has refused his assent to laws the most wholesome and necessary for the public good:

He has forbidden his governors to pass laws of immediate and pressing importance, unless suspended in their operation till his assent should be obtained; and when so suspended, he has neglected utterly to attend to them.

He has refused to pass other laws for the accommodation of large districts of people unless those people would relinquish the right of representation in the legislature, a right inestimable to them and formidable to tyrants only:

He has dissolved Representatives houses repeatedly and continually, for opposing with manly firmness his invasions on the rights of the people:

He has refused for a long space of time to cause others to be elected, whereby the legislative powers, incapable of annihilation, have returned to the people at large for their exercise, the state remaining in the meantime exposed to all the dangers of invasion from without and convulsions within:

He has endeavored to prevent the population of these states; for that purpose obstructing the laws for naturalization for foreigners; refusing to pass others to encourage their migrations hither; and raising the conditions of new appropriations of lands:

He has suffered the administration of justice totally to cease in some of these colonies, refusing his assent to laws for establishing judiciary powers:

He has made our judges dependent on his will alone, for the tenure of their offices, and amount of their salaries:

He has erected a multitude of new offices by a self-assumed power, and sent hither swarms of officers to harass our people and eat out their substance:

He has kept among us in times of peace standing armies and ships of war:

He has affected to render the military, independent of and superior to the civil power:

He has combined with others to subject us to a jurisdiction foreign to our constitutions and unacknowledged by our laws; giving his assent to their pretended acts of legislation, for quartering large bodies of armed troops among us;

For protecting them by a mock-trial from punishment for any murders which they should commit on the inhabitants of these states;

For cutting off our trade with all parts of the world;

For imposing taxes on us without our consent;

For depriving us of the benefits of trial by jury;

For transporting us beyond seas to be tried for pretended offenses;

For taking away our charters, and altering fundamentally the forms of our governments;

For suspending our own legislatures and declaring themselves invested with power to legislate for us in all cases whatsoever:

He has abdicated government here, withdrawing his governors, and declaring us out of his allegiance and protection:

He has plundered our seas, ravaged our coasts, burnt our towns and destroyed the lives of our people:

He is at this time transporting large armies of foreign mercenaries to compleat the works of death, desolation and tyranny, already begun with circumstances of cruelty and perfidy unworthy the head of a civilized nation:

He has endeavored to bring on the inhabitants of our frontiers the merciless Indian savages, whose known rule of warfare is an undistinguished destruction of all ages, sexes, and conditions of existence:

He has incited treasonable insurrections of our fellow citizens, with the allurements of forfeiture and confiscation of our property:

He has waged cruel war against human nature itself, violating its most sacred rights of life and liberty in the persons of a distant people who never offended him, captivating and carrying them into slavery in another hemisphere, or to incur miserable death in their transportation thither. This piratical warfare, the opprobrium of infidels powers, is the warfare of the Christian king of Great Britain. He has prostituted his negative for suppressing every legislative attempt to prohibit or to restrain this execrable commerce determining to keep open a market where MEN should be bought and sold: and that this assemblage of horrors might want no fact of distinguished die, he is now exciting those very people to rise in arms among us, and to purchase that liberty of which he has deprived them, by murdering the people upon whom he also obtruded them: thus paying off former crimes committed against the liberties of one people, with crimes which he urges them to commit against the lives of another.

In every stage of these oppressions we have petitioned for redress in the most humble terms; our repeated petitions have been answered by repeated injury. A prince whose character is thus marked by every act which may define a tyrant, is unfit to be the ruler of a people who mean to be free. Future ages will scarce believe that the hardiness of one man, adventured within the short compass of twelve years only, on so many acts of tyranny without a mask, over a people fostered and fixed in principles of liberty.

Nor have we been wanting in attentions to our British brethren. We have warned them from time to time of attempts by their legislature to extend a jurisdiction over these our states. We have reminded them of the circumstances of our emigration and settlement here, no one of which could warrant so strange a pretension: that these were effected at the expense of our own blood and treasure, unassisted by the wealth or the strength of Great Britain: that in constituting indeed our several forms of government, we had adopted one common king, thereby laying a foundation for perpetual league and amity with them: but that submission to their parliament was no part of our constitution, nor ever in idea, if history may be credited: and we appealed to their native justice and magnanimity, as well as to the ties of our common kindred to disavow these usurpations which were likely to interrupt our correspondence and connection. They too have been deaf to the voice of justice and of consanguinity, and when occasions have been given them, by the regular course of their laws, of removing from their councils the disturbers of our harmony, they have by their free election re-established them in power. At this very time too they are permitting their chief magistrate to send over not only soldiers of our common blood, but Scotch and foreign mercenaries to invade and deluge us in blood. These facts have given the last stab to agonizing affection, and manly spirit bids us to renounce forever these unfeeling brethren. We must endeavor to forget our former love for them, and to hold them as we hold the rest of mankind, enemies in war, in peace friends. We might have been a free and a great people together; but a communication of grandeur and of freedom it seems is below their dignity. Be it so, since they will have it; the road to happiness and to glory is open to all of us too; we will climb it apart from them, and acquiesce in the necessity which denounces our eternal separation!

We therefore the representatives of the United States of America in General Congress assembled do, in the name and by authority of the good people of these states, reject and renounce all allegiance and subjection to the kings of Great Britain and all others who may hereafter claim by, through, or under them; we utterly dissolve and break off all political connection which may have heretofore subsisted between us and the people or parliament of Great Britain; and finally we do assert and declare these colonies to be free and independent states they shall hereafter have full power to levy war, conclude peace, contract alliances, establish commerce, and to do all other acts and things which independent states may of right do. And for the support of this declaration we mutually pledge to each other our lives, our fortunes, and our sacred honour.

WHO'S WHO IN THE DECLARATION

Name and state represented	Date of birth	Place of birth	Age in 1776	Occupation	Date of death
Adams, John, MA	10/30/1735	Quincy, MA	40	Lawyer	7/4/1826
Adams, Samuel, MA	9/27/1722	Boston, MA	53	Merchant	10/2/1803
Bartlett, Josiah, NH	11/21/1729	Amesbury, MA	46	Physician	5/19/1795
Braxton, Carter, VA	9/10/1736	Newington, VA	39	Plantation owner	10/10/1797
Carroll, Charles, MD	9/19/1737	Annapolis, MD	38	Merchant/plantation owner	11/14/1832
Chase, Samuel, MD	4/17/1741	Somerset Co., MD	35	Lawyer	6/19/1811
Clark, Abraham, NJ	2/15/1726	Elizabethtown, NJ	50	Lawyer/surveyor	9/15/1794
Clymer, George, PA	3/16/1739	Philadelphia, PA	37	Merchant	1/24/1813
Ellery, William, RI	12/22/1727	Newport, RI	48	Lawyer/merchant	2/15/1820
Floyd, William, NJ	12/17/1734	Brookhaven, NY	41	Land speculator	8/4/1821
Franklin, Benjamin, PA	1/17/1706	Boston, MA	70	Scientist/printer	4/17/1790
Gerry, Elbridge, MA	7/17/1744	Marblehead, MA	32	Merchant	11/23/1814
Gwinnett, Button, GA	c. 1735	Gloucester, England	41	Merchant/plantation owner	5/15/1777
Hall, Lyman, GA	4/12/1724	Wallingford, CT	52	Physician/minister	10/19/1790
Hancock, John, MA	1/12/1737	Quincy, MA	40	Merchant	10/8/1793
Harrison, Benjamin, VA	4/7/1726	Charles City Co., VA	50	Plantation owner/farmer	4/24/1791
Hart, John, NJ	c. 1711	Hunterdon Co., NJ	65	Land owner	5/11/1779
Hewes, Joseph, NC	1/23/1730	Kingston, NJ	46	Merchant	10/10/1779
Heyward Jr., Thomas, SC	7/28/1746	St. Helena Parish, SC	30	Lawyer/plantation owner	3/6/1809
Hooper, William, NC	6/17/1742	Boston, MA	34	Lawyer	10/14/1790
Hopkins, Stephen, RI	3/7/1707	Providence, RI	69	Merchant	4/13/1785
Hopkinson, Francis, NJ	10/2/1737	Philadelphia, PA	38	Lawyer/musician	5/9/1791
Huntington, Samuel, CT	7/3/1731	Windham, CT	45	Lawyer	1/5/1796
Jefferson, Thomas, VA	4/13/1743	Albemarle Co., VA	33	Lawyer/plantation owner/scientist	7/4/1826
Lee, Francis Lightfoot, VA	10/14/1734	Mt. Pleasant, VA	41	Plantation owner	1/11/1797
Lee, Richard Henry, VA	1/20/1732	Stratford, VA	44	Plantation owner/merchant	6/19/1794
Lewis, Francis, NY	3/21/1713	Llandaff, Wales	63	Merchant	12/30/1802
Livingston, Philip, NY	1/15/1716	Albany, NY	60	Merchant	6/12/1778
Lynch Jr., Thomas, SC	8/5/1749	Prince George's Parish, SC	26	Lawyer	c. 1779
McKean, Thomas, DE	3/19/1735	Chester Co., PA	42	Lawyer	6/24/1817
Middleton, Arthur, SC	6/26/1742	Charleston, SC	34	Plantation owner	1/1/1787
Morris, Lewis, NY	4/8/1726	Westchester Co., NY	50	Plantation owner	1/22/1798
Morris, Robert, PA	1/31/1734	Liverpool, England	42	Merchant/land speculator	5/8/1806
Morton, John, PA	c. 1724	Ridley Township, PA	52	Farmer	c. 1777
Nelson Jr., Thomas, VA	12/26/1738	Yorktown, VA	37	Merchant/plantation owner	1/4/1789
Paca, William, MD	10/31/1740	Abington, MD	35	Lawyer/plantation owner	10/13/1799
Paine, Robert Treat, MA	3/11/1731	Boston, MA	45	Lawyer/scientist	5/12/1814

Name and state represented	Date of birth	Place of birth	Age in 1776	Occupation	Date of death
Penn, John, NC	5/6/1740	Carolina Co., VA	36	Lawyer	9/14/1788
Read, George, DE	9/18/1733	Northeast MD	42	Lawyer	9/21/1798
Rodney, Caesar, DE	10/7/1728	Dover, DE	47	Plantation owner/military officer	6/29/1784
Ross, George, PA	5/10/1730	New Castle, DE	46	Lawyer	7/14/1779
Rush, Benjamin Dr., PA	1/4/1746	Philadelphia, PA	30	Physician	4/19/1813
Rutledge, Edward, SC	11/23/1749	Christ Church Parish, SC	26	Lawyer/plantation owner	1/23/1800
Sherman, Roger, CT	4/19/1721	Newton, MA	55	Lawyer	7/23/1793
Smith, James, PA	c. 1719	Northern Ireland	57	Lawyer	7/11/1806
Stockton, Richard, NJ	10/1/1730	Princeton, NJ	45	Lawyer	2/28/1781
Stone, Thomas, MD	c. 1743	Charles Co., MD	33	Lawyer	10/5/1787
Taylor, George, PA	c. 1716	Ireland	60	Merchant	2/23/1781
Thornton, Matthew, NH	c. 1714	Ireland	62	Physician	6/24/1803
Walton, George, GA	c. 1741	Cumberland Co., VA	35	Lawyer	2/2/1804
Whipple, William, NH	1/14/1730	Kittery, ME	46	Merchant	11/28/1785
Williams, William, CT	4/18/1731	Lebanon, CT	45	Merchant	8/2/1811
Wilson, James, PA	9/14/1742	Carskerdo, Scotland	33	Lawyer	8/21/1798
Witherspoon, John, NJ	2/5/1723	Gifford, Scotland	53	Minister	11/15/1794
Wolcott, Oliver, CT	11/20/1726	Windsor, CT	49	Lawyer	12/1/1797
Wythe, George, VA	c. 1726	Elizabeth City Co., VA	50	Lawyer	6/8/1806

Source: U.S. National Archives and Records Administration

UNDERSTANDING THE DECLARATION OF INDEPENDENCE
GLOSSARY

absolutist A political theory that absolute power should be given to one or more absolute rulers.

aristocracy The upper class, superior in heredity and wealth.

autonomous Existing independently, with the right to self-govern.

emancipation The act of becoming free from the power or control of another.

infrastructure The system of public works including transportation, communication, and waste disposal required for a country or region to run smoothly.

loyalist American colonists who remained loyal to Britain during the fight for American independence.

mercenaries Hired soldiers, usually from a country outside of the conflict.

mores Moral customs.

nationalism Loyalty and devotion to one's country, placing it above all others.

polymath A person who is very well read.

refute To prove incorrect with an argument or evidence.

tabula rasa The idea that the mind is a blank slate before receiving information from outside influences.

theology The study of religion.

utilitarianism The idea that the moral worth of an action is determined by its outcome.

vociferous Given to strong emotional outcry.

UNDERSTANDING THE
DECLARATION OF INDEPENDENCE
FOR MORE INFORMATION

Adams National Historical Park
135 Adams Street
Quincy, MA 02169
(617) 773-1177
Web site: http://www.nps.gov
This national park features the birthplaces
of John Adams and John Quincy Adams.

The Franklin Institute
222 North 20th Street
Philadelphia, PA 19103
(215) 448-1200
Web site: http://www2.fi.edu
The institute is a hands-on science
museum dedicated to great inventors,
including Benjamin Franklin.

The Metropolitan Museum of Art
1000 Fifth Avenue
New York, NY 10028-0198
(212) 535-7710
Web site: http://www.metmuseum.org
Founded in 1870, this is one of the largest
art museums in the world, with more
than two million works of art spanning
five thousand years of world culture.

Monticello
P.O. Box 316

Charlottesville, VA 22902
(434) 984-9822
Web site: http://www.monticello.org
Monticello is the former home of Thomas
Jefferson, now a museum.

National Museum of American History
14th Street and Constitution Avenue NW
Washington, DC, 20560
(202) 633-1000
Web site: http://americanhistory.si.edu
This museum collects and preserves
artifacts from American history.

National Museum of the American
Revolution
Washington Crossing State Park
355 Washington Crossing-Pennington Road
Titusville, NJ 08560
Web site: http://www.
nationalmuseumoftheamericanrevolution.org
The foundation and museum are dedicated to
preserving artifacts and records from the
Revolutionary War.

The Philadelphia History Museum
15 South 7th Street
Philadelphia, PA 19106
(215) 685-4830

Web site: http://philadelphiahistory.org
This newly-renovated museum explores
Philadelphia's history.

The U.S. National Archives and Records
Administration
8601 Adelphi Road
College Park, MD 20740
(866) 272-6272
Web site: http://www.archives.gov
The U.S. National Archives and Records
Administration is the nation's
keeper of all documents and
materials created in the course of
business conducted by the U.S.
government.

Web Sites

Due to the changing nature of Internet
links, Rosen Publishing has developed an
online list of Web sites related to the
subject of this book. This site is updated
regularly. Please use this link to access
the list:

http://www.rosenlinks.com/wtcw/udoi

UNDERSTANDING THE DECLARATION OF INDEPENDENCE
FOR FURTHER READING

Fehrenback, T. R. *Greatness to Spare: The heroic sacrifices of the men who signed the Declaration of Independence*, Princeton, N.J.: D. Van Nostrand & Co., 1968.

Ferling, John. *Setting the World Ablaze: Washington, Adams, Jefferson, and the American Revolution*, Oxford and New York: Oxford University Press, 2000.

Maier, Pauline. *American Scripture*, New York: Alfred A. Knopf, 1998.

Meister, Charles W. *The Founding Fathers*, North Carolina: McFarland & Co., 1987.

Morgan, Edmund S. *Benjamin Franklin*, New Haven: Yale University Press, 2002.

Morison, Samuel Eliot, Commager, Henry Steele, and Leuchtenburg, William E. *The Growth of the American Republic*, New York: Oxford University Press, 1980.

Wills, Garry. *Inventing America: Jefferson's Declaration of Independence*, New York: Doubleday & Co., 1978.

Wood, Gordon S. *The American Revolution: A History*, New York: Modern Library, 2002.

UNDERSTANDING THE
DECLARATION OF INDEPENDENCE
INDEX

UNDERSTANDING THE
DECLARATION OF INDEPENDENCE
ABOUT THE AUTHOR

Stephanie Schwartz Driver is a journalist, writer, and editor. She has written extensively on culture, history, and travel. Recently she has contributed to a new travel guide to New York City and edited a series of books on US immigration.